Ski Well Simply

-- And love skiing more

Contents

Dedicated to my wife Maureen and sons Ben and Darren
who continue willingly to support my endeavors

FOR THE LOVE OF SKIING

Great ski technique frees the skier within, boosts our potential for fun, and saves energy for après ski. The challenge for skiers seeking to improve their skiing is finding a technical model that works well and can be learned quickly. The goal of Ski Well Simply is to describe such a model and how to apply it, and thus to help you along your journey to skiing mastery.

This book assumes that you can already ski, and more importantly, that you are seeking to improve your skiing and your understanding of the sport. Perhaps you can ski easier runs without angst or difficulty, but want to do so with more poise and proficiency. Perhaps you have skied several years but feel stuck at the intermediate level, hesitant to explore places on the mountain that are enticing but beyond your abilities. Or perhaps you are an advanced skier who is capable of descending experts only terrain, but want to improve so you can have more fun for more hours on a given day. Whatever your ability, ski time is precious and you do not want to waste time or money pursuing a myriad of ideas that may or may not advance your on-snow ability.

What is at the core of skiing with confidence, ease, and fun? In a word, simplicity. Simplicity in skiing is possible when our biomechanics are in harmony with the physics at play, producing a synergy that compels our skis to carry us along a desired line of travel at a desired speed for a minimum of effort. Where should we look, what movements and efforts should we make, and what should we feel, in short, what should we *do* so that skiing becomes alive, fun and free?

Ski Well Simply describes in easy to understand terms a method for simple and effective skiing, complete with explanations and rationale for specific how-to's that underpin the method. Whether cruising gently on groomed pistes, plunging through deep powder, bouncing down moguls, or racing around gates, skiing well simply draws on a few insightful techniques and focuses that combine to produce competent, fun skiing in every situation. The method in Ski Well Simply derives from the author's ongoing quest for simple, effective skiing that works anywhere on the mountain, in any snow condition, and at any age. It is distilled from years of all-mountain skiing, training with experts, ski racing, technical skiing, and instructing and coaching beginner through expert level skiers. It is the product of a professional engineer's mind being fully absorbed in seeking a simple solution to a complex and worthy problem.

My journey to this point wasn't simple, but the result is. I'm happy to be part of your journey to lifelong skiing enjoyment, whether it involves simply reading what I've described and thinking about it, or fully following the method and seeing what happens as you personalize it in your skiing. Ski Well Simply is written for easy comprehension by intermediate through expert skiers, as well as instructors and coaches. My wish is that, by reading, visualizing, and trying what it describes, you will improve your skiing and your understanding of skiing, and as a result, enjoy skiing more than ever before.

Ken Chaddock, Whistler, Canada

Ken is a dedicated skiing enthusiast since 1972, now approaching 3,000 days on our two behemoth hills here at Whistler Blackcomb, our revered 'backyard'. I learned to ski as an adult, with my understanding of ski technique deepening significantly in recent years while I transitioned from my career as a professional engineer to a post-retirement phase in ski instructing. The freshness of my learning and my ongoing quest to ski better, and to help others ski better, keeps me focused on the essence of what enables great skiing. My inspiration is the on-hill freedom gained through better skiing, and the joy that people express when they experience new levels in their skiing. Come ski with me! For more information go to www.skiwellsimply.com.

A B C YOUR WAY TO BETTER SKIING

I want my skiing to 'just work'. I seek to be pilot and navigator, unburdened by the workings of the underlying machine, free to choose where to travel and at what speed, then to enjoy the thrill of things playing out as intended. To realize this vision, I want the underlying machine (me) tasked with no more than simple, logical, and effective efforts that yield inspiring skiing.

With simplicity in mind, I want a minimum of focuses to guide my efforts. I use three guiding focuses as a basis of simple and effective skiing, regardless of terrain and snow conditions:

A is for Alignment. Alignment relates to stance, and how we progress our stance so our skis perform turns without us working any harder than necessary. How we arrange and progress our posture significantly influences how effectively our skis turn as well as our ability to resist the forces that arise through our skis and feet while they turn.

B is for Balance. Balance relates what we do and feel in order to remain upright while our skis carry us downhill in a linked set of turns. Standing centered and balanced encourages our skis to behave reliably and predictably, and such behavior helps keep our balancing act as simple as possible.

C is for Coiling. Coiling relates to building and releasing torsion in the body that helps us flow from one turn to the next smoothly and effortlessly. Effective alignment and centered balance lead to effective coiling, which leads to efficient and versatile skiing.

Our method for skiing should allow us to enjoy rhythmic linked turns that we can easily vary in length and frequency in order to adapt to the immediate terrain. While turns may vary in length and cadence, the underlying cycle is a turn then a transition to a subsequent turn, willfully repeated.

Align-Balance-Coil names the three guiding focuses that repeat with each turn cycle in the Ski Well Simply model. These focuses guide our movements and efforts turn to turn, while the feedback we feel up through our feet signals our level of success. Alignment is the guiding focus between turns, where we prepare our stance for the increase in underfoot pressure that will accompany the turn. Balance becomes the guiding focus throughout the turn, while we use a progressive stance to encourage our skis to perform the turn predictably and reliably. Coiling becomes the guiding focus late in the turn and through release from the turn, and helps us flow into the next turn smoothly and seamlessly. Figure 1 illustrates the three guiding focuses and where each is most prominent in the turn cycle.

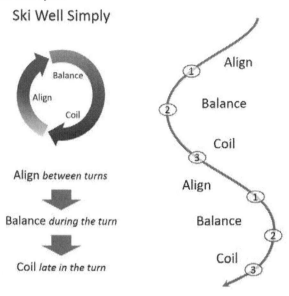

Figure 1. The Ski Well Simply method produces simple, effective skiing. It has three guiding focuses, Alignment, Balance and Coiling, and three points within the turn cycle for assessing movements, efforts, and sensations: (1) at the start of the turn, (2) at mid turn, and (3) at release from the turn.

The focuses of alignment, balance, and coiling overlap and morph one into the next as we ski turn to turn. We achieve smooth flowing skiing when success with one focus leads to success with the next. For example, coiling builds torsion in the body during a turn, and that torsion helps us flow between turns into an aligned stance that compels our skis to start the next turn. Our alignment at the start of the turn (point 1 in Figure 1) evolves naturally into an effective mid turn geometry in which we are centered and balanced while the skis perform the turn. From mid turn (point 2) our progressing stance geometry and balance facilitate coiling and building torsion in the body through the latter part of the turn. Release from the turn (point 3) then frees the coiled torsion to help us align and prepare for the next turn, and the cycle repeats. Align-Balance-Coil is a model that I use to ski well, and simply.

The upcoming sections describe ALIGNMENT, BALANCE, and COILING in depth. The subsequent section titled BLENDING describes a cue to help us optimize the timing of our movements and efforts. This section includes common difficulties with putting things into practice and developmental drills for building related skills. The final section titled INSIGHTS delves more deeply into specifics that contribute to skiing well simply for further understanding. Let's start with the three guiding focuses.

ALIGNMENT

<u>What is Alignment and Why is it Important?</u>

Alignment relates to the arrangement of our skeleton in order to minimize our effort to stand and balance. When skiing, we experience changes in how much we weigh while our line of travel progresses from turn to turn. Generally, we feel lightest between turns, and heaviest mid to late in each turn, where forces push up through our skis and feet to curve our line of travel away from the line that momentum and gravity would otherwise dictate. The induced weight we experience turn to turn can vary significantly. At gentler speeds, our weight remains close to our static weight, which is the weight we have when we stand still on a bathroom scale. At higher speeds, and tighter turns, our induced weight can peak at several times our static weight, then drop between turns to as little as zero. Our alignment can mean the difference between our muscles being occupied primarily with stabilizing and balancing, or doing that plus working hard to resist peaks in our induced weight. The more we use the alignment of our bones rather than strength of our muscles to resist our weight, the more we can be relaxed and ready to make athletic movements: effective alignment minimizes our muscular effort while freeing us to move and adapt to terrain changes. Figure 2 depicts the different magnitudes of weight that can occur by mid to late in a given turn.

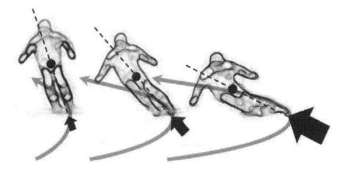

Figure 2. Our induced weight at the apex of a turn can range from one to several gravity equivalents depending on speed of travel and sharpness of turn, as depicted by the size of the arrow in each of the above images. An effective alignment involves a neutral untwisted spine and an outside leg with little enough bend in the knee to withstand the weight of the turn.

Alignment also relates to the geometry of our stance. Our stance geometry is essentially set by the angle at the hinge point between upper and lower body, where torso meets upper legs or pelvis meets femurs, namely the hip joints. Whatever the angle at our hip joints, we instinctively adjust other body parts to pursue and achieve balance. Notably, adjusting hip angle simultaneously affects how well the skis grip and the tightness of turn they make, and our ability to maintain our stance amid the increase in weight that we experience during the turn.

Good alignment is a leading contributor to simple, effective, efficient skiing, and enjoying solid ski performance with a minimum of effort. A well-aligned stance at the start of the turn contributes to effective balancing and coiling through the rest of the turn. The upcoming sections titled BALANCE and COILING will highlight the role of alignment and postural geometry as the turn progresses. For now, the immediate focus is on alignment in preparation for the start of the turn.

Some Reference Terminology

In order to help describe alignment, let's introduce some terminology that will be used throughout the book.

Outside foot: the foot that travels the perimeter of the turn and becomes the downhill foot at the end of a turn. Similarly for outside boot, outside ski, outside arm, outside pole, etc.

Magic Carpet: an imaginary platform on which we stand and balance. The magic carpet is a small rectangular area about the size of a carpet sample, just large enough to encircle our boots and bindings, about one and half boot lengths long and about three boot widths wide. Holding our feet parallel to each other and 'on the magic carpet' improves our ability to balance and adapt to terrain changes—we get a 'magic carpet ride', hence the moniker. Note: magic carpet often refers to a carpeted ski lift that beginners stand on to ride uphill in learner zones. In this book, magic carpet means a small imaginary carpet that skilled skiers stand on to ride downhill, in any zone.

Belly Button Laser Beam: an external cue related to the geometry of stance. Imagine a laser beam shining straight out of your belly button, ahead and above the slope. The laser shines in a direction that reveals the direction of your pelvis, a useful insight as will become apparent later in the book. Get your beam on.

Powerhouse: our foundation for movements and efforts while skiing. The powerhouse comprises the lower torso, hip joints, and upper legs, essentially everything between the ribs and the knees. This portion of the body contains significant mass and strength, and contains the hip joints, where the angles we choose largely determines how our skis turn and our ability to withstand the weight induced by their turns. The mass, mobility and strength in the powerhouse makes it central to how our skiing works: just as having our house in order implies living well wisely, having our powerhouse in order underlies skiing well simply.

How to Align Between Turns

Alignment is the guiding focus after release from one turn until the start of the next. Figure 3 shows where during the turn cycle we should focus on getting our stance aligned and ready for the upcoming turn.

Effective alignment at the start of the turn means standing relaxed and ready for the turn to develop, balancing and letting the skis begin to shape the turn. This encourages a smooth flow into the turn and is the start of a progression in stance that continues throughout the turn. There are several contributors to moving through an effective skiing-purposed alignment as the skis begin the turn. These contributors are the same regardless of terrain or skiing situation, whether it's deep powder, moguls, slow skidded turns, or fast carved turns.

1) Where to look. Late in a turn, visualize the line along which you expect your skis will carry you early in the upcoming turn. Seeing in advance where you intend to travel helps you align and prepare appropriately (and automatically), and greatly increases the odds that you will get to enjoy the turn you intend.

2) What effort or movement to make. Between turns is where most of our movement, or change in stance, occurs. Good management of alignment and stance during the previous turn will have produced an increase in apparent weight, followed by a temporary drop in weight during the transition to the next turn. Being lighter for a brief instant allows us to extend our legs while our skis begin to pick up the new turn, after which our weight increases again. While light, feet are best held parallel and side by side on the magic carpet, with knees as far apart as the skis, and both extended a little towards the outside of the new turn. As the turn approaches, extend your legs, in particular your outside leg,

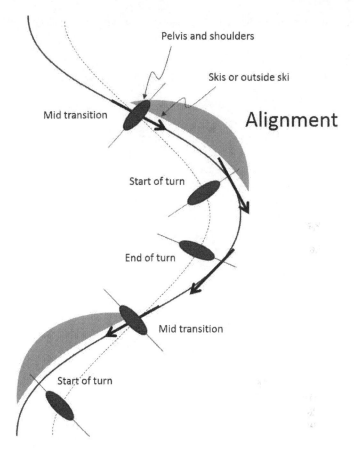

Figure 3. Alignment is a key focus to guide movements after mid transition and en route to the next turn.

and patiently allow the skis to pick up the new turn – be patient: think "balance", rather than "turn". Align your upper body to itself, with the pelvis as its reference: shoulders parallel to pelvis, arms extended ahead and out to the sides with elbows slightly bent, and spine neutral rather than hunched, arched or twisted. Note that this arrangement of shoulders, arms, spine and pelvis is the target alignment for the upper body throughout the whole turn cycle. The upper body is tilted forward more than it would be when standing in ski boots in a lift line or a cafeteria, with more bend forward at the hip joints, ready for action. Figure 4 summarizes these points.

3) What to feel. Seek to feel pressure along the arch side of the outside foot, with the ball through heel engaged and carrying weight. To confirm being centered, seek equal pressure from the tongue and back cuff of your boots against your shins and calves. Use no more tension than necessary throughout your body to provide structure to your stance; some tension is required to maintain your alignment while sliding over or through changes in the snow height and depth, but too much tension will interfere with your ability to move and adapt to the terrain. Standing centered without excessive tension also allows the skis to flow into the new turn unhindered by the effects of an overly braced passenger.

Standing balanced as such with legs extended, wait patiently for the skis to start to turn. Do as little else as possible, unless, of course, a surprise or mishap occurs; in that case, not to worry, you'll do whatever comes naturally...

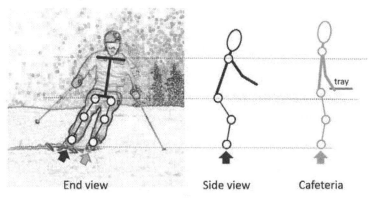

End view   Side view   Cafeteria

Figure 4. Target alignment during approach to the turn. The amount of bend in the hip joints should be more than what you would use when standing in ski boots holding a cafeteria tray.

How much we extend between turns is a tradeoff between alignment of torso and legs to help withstand the induced weight of the upcoming turn, and, shock absorption to ride smoothly over bumps and ripples in the snow. Retaining a little bend at the hip joints keeps our powerhouse poised where we can tense quickly to preserve our stance amid sudden spikes in weight, or flex or extend as needed to help deal with nuances and challenges that arise during the turn. Figures 5(a), 5(b), and 5(c) relate to these points.

Figure 5(a). Extended stance, just as the skis begin the turn, when cruising at speed.

Figure 5(a) shows entry to the turn. Here I am balanced in a ready athletic posture with a little forward bend in the hip joints, patiently letting my skis pick up the turn. Note the relationship of the upper body to itself: arms symmetrical, shoulders parallel to pelvis, hence lower arms and hands symmetrical to pelvis. This is the target relationship for the upper body throughout the whole turn cycle, beginning with alignment between turns. The pelvis faces the direction of travel, as the belly button laser attests (note the arrow). The upper body is near perpendicular to the slope laterally, which keeps the outside pole tip near the snow. The feet directly under me on the magic carpet provides a solid platform on which to enter and ride the turn. My head facing slightly towards the inside of the turn reveals that I am looking ahead, judging snow conditions and predicting my line of travel from the middle through the end of the turn. Looking ahead allows me to plan and then progress my stance in accordance with my objectives for the turn and what I predict it will produce in terms of the change in line of travel and underfoot pressure.

Figure 5(b). Extended tall, for a patient instant, in moguls.

Figure 5(b) shows the same point in the turn cycle, at entry to the turn, in moguls. Note the extended stance in anticipation of a sharp increase in weight when I encounter the trough and mogul that is just ahead of me. Feet on the magic carpet, upper body aligned to itself, and torso facing the direction of travel all help me be ready to deal with, or play with, the immediate action that awaits.

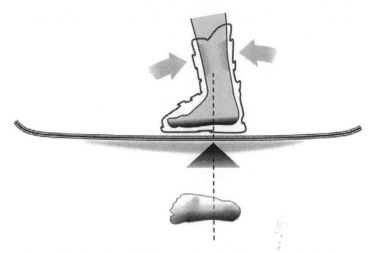

Figure 5(c). Pressure distribution on the sole of the outside foot and on the shin and calf of the outside leg early in the turn. Darker shading indicates greater pressure.

Figure 5(c) depicts what I seek to feel from my outside boot as the turn begins. Standing with a good portion of my weight centered on the arch side of the outside foot contributes ski grip and encourages the skis to begin the turn. Pressure distributed ball through heel and pressure equal on shin and calf confirms that my weight is acting downwards through the middle of the ski, so it is most likely to perform the turn with the fewest possible surprises.

Perfection at the Start of the Turn

The skis begin the turn while we do nothing more than stand ready and balance patiently, feeling much of our weight along the arch side of the outside foot.

Alignment Do's and Don'ts as the Turn Develops

As the turn develops, the skis engage and curve our line of travel. While this happens, we evolve our stance in a way that compels our skis to perform the turn, with whatever mix of carving, skidding and slipping we intend, in return for us continuing to stand centered and balanced. The next section will deal with balance in depth. In the meantime, it is worth emphasizing one 'must do' and one 'must not do' while the turn develops, to ensure that our alignment evolves in a way that compels our skis to perform the turn we intend.

First, the 'must do'. Be sure that the legs turn sooner than and more than the pelvis does while the skis progress into and through the turn. Success in this regard will result in an oblique angle between where the skis point and where the pelvis faces, that is, between where the skis point and where the belly button laser beam shines. This obliqueness enhances ski grip and facilitates coiling later in the turn.

Now, the 'must not do'. Avoid rotating the upper body into the direction of the turn, as depicted in the right image in Figure 6. Where we intend the upcoming turn to begin may be quickly approaching or worse, already here(!), triggering a natural instinct to try to force our skis to change direction. This triggers twisting the upper body into the direction of the turn in order to force the skis into that same direction. This is commonly called 'rotation', turning the upper body in order to force the skis to change direction. This gross and unsightly move overrides what the skis would otherwise do given their tilt and grip, as influenced by our stance geometry plus centered weight. Rotating the upper body also disrupts balance and flow, and is a very high-effort low-reward method of attempting a turn.

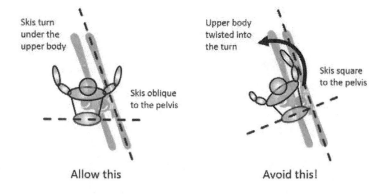

Figure 6. Top view of what to allow during the turn, namely, that the feet turn under the upper body, versus what not to do: turning the upper body into the direction of the turn and losing the desired obliqueness between pelvis and skis.

A basic premise for skiing well simply is that balancing, and only balancing, while progressing our stance through well-chosen skiing-purposed postures compels our skis to perform turns that we intend. Seeking steady balance while turning the legs and feet in sync with the turning action of the skis leads to a natural evolution of our stance geometry with each turn. Figure 7 shows obliqueness developing between the direction of the pelvis and the direction of the skis from the start to the middle of the turn.

Geometry evolves with the turn, guided by balance and the turning action of the skis. If we keep the upper body oriented so the outside pole tip hovers near the snow and focus on a steady distribution of weight along the outside foot, the skis perform the turn predictably. That predictability frees our mind to plan ahead to upcoming turns while we flow through the immediate turn. With the turn progressing, our focus morphs from alignment to balance, the second guiding focus in the Ski Well Simply model.

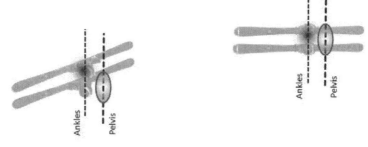

Figure 7. Alignment at the start of the turn and at mid turn. Stance geometry evolves naturally with the pursuit of steady balance and turning the legs and feet to track the changing direction of the skis as they flow into mid turn. Note that the direction of the pelvis changes little if any during this time and the obliqueness is a result of the skis and feet turning under a quiet upper body. Also, note that while the pelvis is oblique to the direction of the feet, it is square in terms of where the feet are located; the feet are under the upper body where you'd expect, but they are both turned a little as a result of having followed the changing direction of the skis.

BALANCE

<u>What Does Balance Mean, Particularly at Mid Turn?</u>

From physics, we are in balance when our weight vector dissects our center of mass and our center of pressure. When our what dissects our what and our what...!?? Let's look at a diagram and to help explain this.

Figure 8. Relationship of weight vector, center of mass, and center of pressure when weight is centered and balanced at mid turn. Our weight vector always acts through our center of pressure, but may miss the center of mass; whenever this occurs we begin to fall and must do something to correct our balance.

In Figure 8 the weight vector is shown as the long diagonal line. This is the direction in which our weight at any instant acts downwards through our body and towards the snow. When in perfect balance, our center of mass and our center of pressure will be along this line. Our center of mass is an imagined compression of all the mass of our body, clothing and equipment into a small sphere, say, the size of a tennis ball. It is usually near our belt buckle, just below our navel, when we stand with some forward bend in the hip joints. Our center of pressure is a point somewhere within and between the soles of our feet where all of our weight can be considered to be concentrated. I like to think of the center of pressure being about the size of a golf ball: small for purposes of precision, yet not so small that balancing on it becomes unimaginably painful (you get the point...). In Figure 8, the tip of the upwards arrow shows where the center of pressure is.

While skiing, or actually any time we are standing and balanced, where we feel pressure on the soles of our feet tells us where our center of pressure is. For example, if all of our weight is on one foot, our center of pressure is somewhere within the area of the sole of that foot. If we feel most of the pressure on the heel of that foot, then our center of pressure is under that one heel. Where the center of pressure should be in order to ski well simply is worth careful consideration.

Generic Challenges to Balance During Every Turn

An effective balancing strategy helps us deal with challenges that are generic to every turn. Understanding these challenges helps identify what needs doing in order to balance effectively.

First, there is loading, or an increase in how heavy we feel, and in fact are, during a turn. Whenever our skis curve our line of travel, our apparent weight increases. The greater our speed, the greater our momentum, and thus the greater the weight we need to be able to balance in the presence of. When my line of travel curves sharply, my weight typically climbs to anywhere between one and a half to three times what it is when I am standing still at zero speed. As an interesting aside, this means that my legs, and mainly my outside leg, may need to withstand several hundred pounds of load at the apex of each turn; no wonder I feel the way I do at the end of a good day of skiing! Loading may peak for half a second or less in a short turn, and for a second or more in a long turn. Effective alignment helps us maintain our stance amid the loading of the turn, and transmits our increased weight down through our skis so they keep turning as predicted.

Second, our skis must grip the snow in order to perform a turn, our task being to control the amount of grip in order to achieve what we want. Grip refers to a ski's reluctance to slip sideways relative to the direction it is pointed in. More grip results when our weight presses one edge more deeply into the snow than the other edge; the skis will tend to turn in the direction they are tilted towards. Notably, how we arrange our stance can affect the tilt of the skis and thus how readily the skis grip and change direction. The linkage between grip and how we stand or move while standing might be considered a challenge, although is more an opportunity to exploit in order to achieve simpler skiing. More on this subject later.

Third, the snow during a turn may change in firmness, height, and friction. Dealing with such changes calls for robust balance. Standing in a manner that promotes stability yet keeps us free to move and react quickly adds robustness to our balancing act. When we align so that our skeleton bears most of our weight, it takes less effort to stabilize and leaves more freedom for reflexes and movements that add playfulness in our skiing. Figure 9 highlights where in the turn cycle balance should be foremost in our focus.

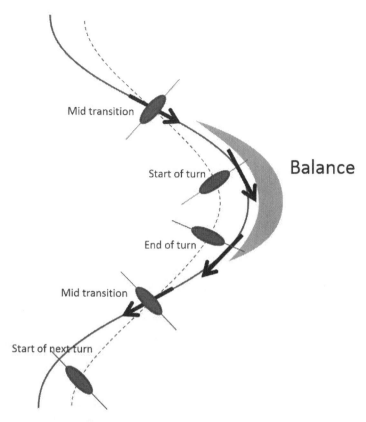

Figure 9. Balance becomes the leading focus through the heart of the turn, where underfoot pressures can peak well above regular body weight, and remaining centered is critical to the turn progressing as planned.

The Role of Balance in Skiing

"It's our job to balance and our skis' job to turn" is a saying I return to again and again. To me, skiing is an act of dynamic standing rather than an act of turning. I want my turns to result from the geometry of my stance and the quality of my balance, rather than due to me swiveling, twisting, or pivoting my skis into a particular direction. I want to arrange my stance according to the turn I intend my skis to make, then balance and enjoy the turn they make, moving within a postural range that is manageable amid the loading of the turn. Success is having my skis perform the turn I planned, whether carving a clean arc, skidding to control speed, or slipping and surfing into a turn, in return for me standing centered and balanced while they do so. Please note that use of the word 'standing' in no way implies 'static'; more about how the geometry of my stance progresses throughout the turn is presented a few sections ahead.

Balancing can be pursued in a variety of ways, and can be simple or complex depending on the efforts and movements used. To ski well simply, I want a balancing act that is simple. I also want to have my skis turn as intended. What are the contributors to a simple balancing act that compels our skis to turn as we intend them to?

Balance relies on our balancing mechanisms (eyesight, vestibular system, proprioception, etc.) to be in good working order. General health and fitness are key factors in how well these mechanisms are working. Assuming these mechanisms are just fine, the balancing process starts with looking smart, or rather, being smart about where we look.

To help balance, we want to pinpoint the line that we aim to travel within the next few seconds. What we see and what we predict will happen based on what we see subconsciously guides our actions, so looking where we want to travel, and not looking where we don't want to travel, is sound advice. For example, skiing through the trees really means skiing between the trees. So, look at the spaces between the trees where you want to travel rather than at the trees where you don't want to travel. Of course, if you do encounter a tree head on, you can always sum up at après, "I wondered why that tree looked so big...and then it hit me!"

I must emphasize that looking only where you are about to travel is less than safe if that's the only place you look. To be safe, be sure to watch all around for potential hazards, especially moving hazards such as other sliders and riders who are less skilled or more reckless than they should be, and snowmobiles and grooming machines that pass nearby.

My visual process is to scan ahead to choose a general route, narrow my attention to the next two or three turns, then study closely the immediate snow that my skis will encounter as I enter a turn. As I enter the turn, I have a good idea of where I want it to finish and where I want the subsequent turn to begin. This gives me a specific target that guides my actions in order to exit the turn in a favorable direction. Notably, I look ahead, not down. Looking ahead provides better information about where level is, and how the pitch of the upcoming terrain might affect my line of travel. How far ahead? I look ahead at least one 'reaction interval', the time and distance within which I am able to alter my line of travel. Knowing what's coming within an interval in which I can react or adjust allows me to play with, deal with, or avoid whatever I am about to encounter.

Biomechanically, balance means standing with minimal body sway on a chosen center of pressure. Balancing is a dynamic and continuous act that keeps us upright on a shifting center of pressure, whether shifting because of outside influences or our own actions. The better balanced we are, the smaller the area that our center of pressure shifts within if we could observe directly downwards along the line that our weight is acting (our weight vector). Consider what happens when riding a bicycle. Being able to ride a straight line without doing anything to rebalance means being in perfect balance; highly unlikely. More likely is some continual balancing by steering side to side, with less steering the better our balance is. When skiing, the better our balance is the smaller the area within which we feel our center of pressure move while we romp down the hill.

The question is where should we target our center of pressure to be in order to ski well simply? When walking, our center of pressure moves forward with each step, from the heel toward the toes. When skiing, our center of pressure can be virtually anywhere as long as we have the agility to recover and steady our balance before falling becomes a certainty. A high level of agility makes it possible to pull off amazing recoveries and even shift the center of pressure around at will, skiing in and out of balance on purpose. While such intentional shifting can help us develop our balancing skills and become comfortable with being a little out of balance from time to time, skiing in and out of balance with every turn isn't a prerequisite for skiing well simply.

To keep things simple, I use a balance goal that is easy to understand, do, and feel, and is very effective in having my skis do what I intend them to. That goal: keep the center of pressure on my outside foot steady and unchanging throughout the whole of each turn. Why this goal? Read on.

The foot, the whole foot, and nothing but the foot

For standing, the foot is designed to balance with weight mainly shared on the ball and heel of the foot, assisted by proprioception that triggers balancing reflexes upwards through the body. The foot incorporates a transverse arch across the ball of the foot, and a primary arch from the ball and heel that adds weight-bearing strength to the foot. Body weight is supported through the tibia, the primary bone of the lower leg, which rests near the middle of the primary arch. The lower leg is encased in a relatively stiff restrictive ski boot that adds structure and stability but reduces the ease and range of ankle flex. The overall structure is akin to a three-point walking stick with a wee bit of flex where the shaft adjoins the base. Figures 10(a) and 10(b) depict these points.

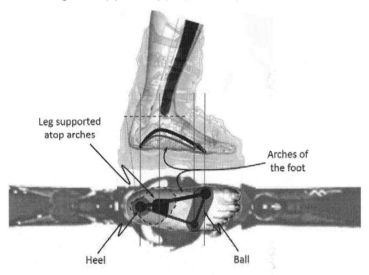

Figure 10(a). Our support structure while skiing begins with the sole of the foot. The sole has two main support areas, the heel, under the heel bone, and the ball of the foot, under the metatarsal joints. The foot structure has three arches, the regularly referred to 'arch' of the foot from the heel to the first metatarsal (behind the big toe), and two lesser arches, one from the heel to the fifth metatarsal, and the other between the first and fifth metatarsals. The foot supports the tibia and lower leg which are enwrapped by the ski boot cuff, poised to lever the ski boot side to side as affected by our overall stance.

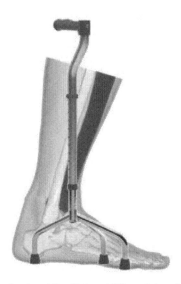

Figure 10(b). The heel and the first and fifth metatarsal joints under the ball of the foot offer a tripod-like base of support. Pressure shared over all three points offers the largest possible surface area on which to balance. During a turn, the skier's weight is mainly shared by the heel, arch and first metatarsal joint. The ski boot helps hold the ski tilted during the turn, in combination with the skier balancing with most of their weight along the arch side of the foot and thus in the inside edge of the ski.

To take advantage of this structure, my balancing strategy during a turn is to feel pressure from the ball through the heel of the foot, and equal pressure from my boot cuffs against the shin and calf of my lower legs. My goal is to rely on my boot cuffs only to help tilt my skis (by levering them side to side as driven by lateral orientation of my lower legs), rather than to lean into in order to balance. After all, ski boots weren't around when humans learned to stand and walk. Standing on the soles of the feet with weight equally shared between ball and heel ensures that whatever weight is on a given foot is centered in the fore and aft direction, in line with the weight bearing structure of my lower leg.

When my weight stays centered as such, my skis perform predictably and reliably. Every ski has a turning center, a point near the middle or waist of the ski that the ski's designer expected the skier's weight to press down through during a turn. When the skier's weight presses through the ski's turning center, the ski reacts with few surprises, and fewer surprises makes for simpler balancing. The turning center of a ski is usually directly under a corresponding mark on the sole of the ski boot when it is clamped into the ski binding. Success with feeling 'the foot, the whole foot, and nothing but the foot' becomes synonymous with a predictable response from my skis and keeps my balancing act as simple as possible.

Balancing where my body is designed to carry weight, on the soles of my feet, also saves my shins from unnecessary abuse. When I teach balancing on the soles of the feet only, students often remark how sore their shins usually get from skiing, but not today! I suspect their history with sore shins is due to having been told to ski with their shins pressed forward into their boot cuffs. From some sources, pressing the shins into the fronts of the boots is a necessary part of pressuring the tip of the ski so that it turns. Unfortunately, this common misguidance leads to sore shins and unsteady skiing. Ask yourself, how do your shins feel at the end of a day of skiing? Have you ever fled early to après-ski because of excessively sore shins?

With the foot used in a good weight-bearing manner, we have the choice to put all of our weight on one foot. Generally, the best approach is to have most of the weight on the outside foot. But what does 'most weight' mean? The answer depends on the situation; generally, the firmer the snow, the higher percentage of weight on the outside foot. In soft snow and deep powder, or during compressions in moguls, near equal weight has an advantage. Whatever the situation, I focus on what I feel on my outside foot and lower leg. I seek to have the pressure distribution on the sole of my outside foot, or, where my center of pressure is on my outside foot, stay constant throughout the turn. I don't pay much attention to my inside foot or leg, other than keeping the skis parallel and the knees as far apart as the skis. Doing so keeps both skis tilted about the same, and minimizes disturbances due to underfoot turbulence that affects the amount of pressure on a given ski. A constant pressure distribution along my outside foot is helpful biofeedback that confirms I am in balance, and helps keep things simple. Figure 11 helps convey these points.

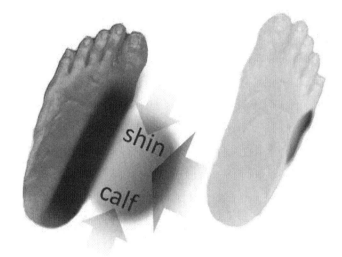

Figure 11. The sensations I seek from my boots during a turn. My goal throughout each turn is to feel a steady pressure pattern on the sole of my outside foot and near equal pressures on the shin and calf of my outside leg. Pursuing a steady center of pressure on the outside foot indirectly guides how much pressure to carry on the inside foot, since some pressure on the inside foot helps achieve a steady pressure pattern on the outside foot.

You might ask how exactly is it possible to stay centered on your feet without leaning against your boot cuffs, given all the underfoot turbulence that arises when skiing. Doesn't balancing on a pair of slippery skis, especially in the fore and aft direction in which they are always slippery, require an inherent ability that we either do or don't have? What exactly can we do to keep our weight centered in the fore and aft direction?

Plantar Tension

If we are to keep our weight solely on our feet (ahem) rather than partially on the cuffs of our boots, we need a means to hold our feet centered in the fore and aft direction. Key to achieving this is plantar tension.

Plantar what(?!) you say... Plantar tension is common in everyday living. We use plantar tension with every step we take, pressing down on the ball of the foot as we roll forward and then step onto the other foot's heel. Plantar tension contributes to plantar flexion, or straightening the ankle to point the toes down and away from the shin. In ski boots, plantar flexion is futile because the boots are too stiff to allow more than very minor flexing of the ankle. Plantar tension, though, is fair game.

To explore the related effort, stand with feet flat on the floor, then raise yourself onto the balls of your feet. Rising up as such recruits plantar tension. Alternatively, think of pressing down on a gas pedal that has been bolted into a fixed position and can't be moved, just like the foot beds in your ski boots. The amount of plantar tension, even without actually flexing the ankle, readily affects the amount of weight on the balls versus the heels of the feet. This effort provides a simple, quick and non-disruptive means to engage the whole foot, ball through heel, and to fine tune where our center of pressure is along the soles of our feet in the fore and aft direction. See Figure 12.

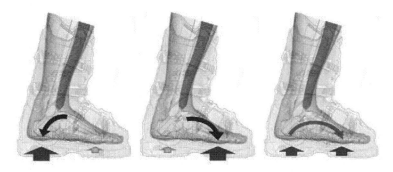

Figure 12. Plantar tension allows modulating the pressure on the ball of the foot versus the heel, as a quick and simple means to center our balance fore and aft. From left to right, too much pressure on the heel; too much pressure on the ball; equal pressure on the ball and heel. Equal pressure ensures that our weight presses down through the middle of the ski, promoting reliable and predictable turning action, which makes it easier to keep centered and balanced.

The time to adjust plantar tension is while aligning to prepare for the upcoming turn, before the skis turn and loading increases. Use just enough plantar tension to equalize the pressure from your boot cuffs on the shin and calf of both legs, and to feel most of your weight from the ball through the heel on the arch side of the outside foot. Centered as such early in the turn dramatically increases the likelihood of centered balance throughout the turn. There's more that we can do to contribute to solid balance in the turn, however, as follows.

<u>Feet on the Magic Carpet</u>

I establish balance using plantar tension to ensure the whole of my outside foot is engaged ball through heel as an integral part of alignment. Standing balanced with pressure centered on the foot, the whole foot, and nothing but the foot is made easier when I keep both feet on the magic carpet. My feet directly under me and on the magic carpet early in the turn helps ensure that I will remain balanced and centered throughout the turn.

While the turn develops, I turn my feet and legs to match the changing direction of my skis under me. By mid turn my skis are oblique to the direction of my pelvis, not because I have forced them to point as such, but because I have turned my feet and legs to follow their change in direction. Turning my feet while keeping them within the magic carpet leads to my inside ski being a little ahead of my outside ski, usually by half a boot length or so. This offset between the ski tips, which is the same for the feet since they are clamped to my skis, allows obliqueness between skis and pelvis to develop freely without requiring any twist in the spine. I want to avoid twisting of the spine because of heavy loading that may accompany the turn, and a twisted loaded spine would invite injury. If both feet were to remain exactly side by side during the turn (like on a mono ski), I would have to contort in the mid-section and spine in order to accommodate a difference in the directions of my skis and upper body, and likely trigger a multiday back ache.

I've seen people who followed to a tee the instructions "keep your upper body facing down the hill" and "feel the pinch" without any guidance as to how to bend safely, using the significant mobility that is inherent in their hip joints. I see them bending at the waist (above the pelvis) rather than at the hip joints (below the pelvis). They've learned to feel their turns, literally, for days. Fortunately, there's a better way.

Using the range of movement inherent in the hip joint to allow the legs and feet to turn under the pelvis achieves a safer and stronger stance amid the loading of the turn, so is what I am careful to do and teach.

Figure 13 depicts the relative position of the feet between turns and during a turn.

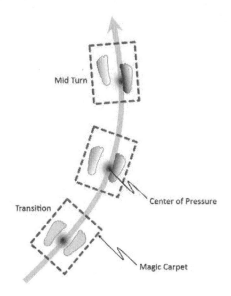

Figure 13. Relative position of the feet on the magic carpet and target location of the center of pressure from mid transition to mid turn, viewed along the weight vector. Shading signifies pressure distribution on the soles of the feet, darker for higher pressure.

Using the magic carpet imagery helps me balance more reliably, and to keep my center of pressure within a small target area. I focus on how my outside foot feels, aiming to feel the whole foot engaged ball through heel, and the center of pressure on its sole steady, shifting neither fore nor aft, throughout the turn. This focus encourages more weight on the outside foot than the inside foot, and minimizes the chance of getting caught lazily standing too much on the inside foot.

How much weight is on the outside foot versus the inside foot seems to sort itself out automatically. Big compressions when skiing moguls or the absence of a firm underfoot surface when floating in deep powder naturally encourages closer to equal weight on both feet. On groomed runs, most weight migrates to the outside foot, more so the firmer the snow. On ice, having virtually all weight on the outside ski maximizes the pressure per inch of ski edge and encourages the best edge penetration and grip possible given the challenging hardness of that condition. I find that seeking a goal of pressure centered and steady along the sole of the outside foot throughout the turn contributes to successful balancing, regardless of how much weight is actually on that foot versus the inside foot.

My feet on the magic carpet works wonders in every situation I encounter, whether it is slow gentle turns, powder and moguls, or fast carved turns and racing. Like magic! The magic carpet is my personal platform on which to balance and ride. And to keep things simple.

Mid Turn Geometry

Let's do a brief exercise to explore what geometry will allow us, with a minimum of effort, to withstand the loading of the turn and at the same time compel our skis to grip and perform the turn. If you stand next to a box of apples (or a case of wine if you prefer) on the floor that is a little off to one side, how should you move in order to lift the box with minimum risk to hurting your back? Assume the box has handles at knee height so you can grab it without bending deeply.

The easiest and safest approach is to face the box with your pelvis and upper body, then bend forward at the hip joints while keeping your spine neutral, that is, without hunching your back. Turning your upper body to face the load is quite easy if you move your feet, but picture that you have skis on and swiveling the skis isn't really an option. In this case, sliding one foot a little ahead of the other so both heels are the same distance from the box makes it much easier for your pelvis to face the box. One foot a little ahead represents what happens when we turn our feet and legs to accommodate the changing direction of our skis during a turn; the pelvis becomes oblique to the feet in terms of direction, but square to the feet in terms of position. It's akin to standing at a squat rack with both feet turned in the same direction while the upper body, pelvis up through shoulders, remains square to the rack.

Since stiff boots inhibit flexing in the ankles, bending to grab the box means flexing mostly at the hip joints. A little flex in the knees occurs naturally in order to keep our center of pressure steady while the hips flex, and a little bend at the knees assists with absorbing ripples and nuances in the passing snow.

This exercise of flexing forward at the hip joints with both feet turned to the left mimics an effective mid turn geometry for a turn to the left; mirror that for a turn to the right. For a revealing contrast stand with your pelvis in the same direction as your feet, and turn only your shoulders when bending towards the box. Ouch! You've just experienced what I've been coached to do many times (but have wisely refused) which is to 'feel the pinch', especially by flexing the spine sideways to 'pinch' the stomach muscles between the edge of the rib cage and the corner of the pelvis. Thankfully, we can use the body in a much safer manner: bending forward at the hip joints when the legs are turned relative to the pelvis. Doing so creates effective angles at the hip joint that drive ski grip with a safe and strong stance suited to resist the induced weight of the turn. Figure 14 summarizes the relationship of the pelvis, feet and imaginary box of apples.

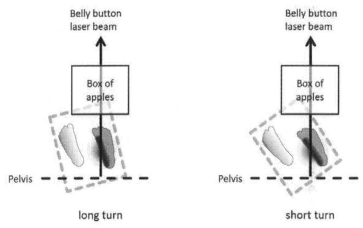

Figure 14. The box of apples analogy during a turn, looking downwards. The feet turned under the pelvis encourages ski grip, since progressively bending forward at the hip joints during the turn not only helps stay balanced but also adds tilt to the skis. More obliqueness between skis and pelvis means more tilt of the skis for a given increase in bend forward at the hip joints. When skiing, the pelvis and skis are less oblique the longer the turn, and more oblique the shorter the turn.

At entry to the turn, we stand aligned with feet near straight ahead relative to the pelvis and most of our weight along the arch side of the outside boot, waiting patiently for the turn to begin. By mid turn, the feet and legs have turned with the skis so the belly button laser beam shoots across the outside ski at a point somewhere between the ski tip and binding toe-piece. At the same time, deflection of our line of travel transforms momentum into weight, increasing how heavy we are and feel. As when lifting or holding a heavy object, safe bending and lifting calls for ensuring that the pelvis faces towards where the upper body is being pulled, which when skiing, is along our line of momentum, usually a little towards the outside of the turn.

As the turn progresses, our geometry evolves to a mid turn geometry, with the outside pole tip near the snow, upper body aligned to itself, and legs turning with the skis, sooner than and more than the pelvis. From mid to late in the turn, maintaining balance on a steady center of pressure leads to increasing forward flex at the hip joints which increases ski grip and facilitates coiling. Figure 15 illustrates the various elements in an effective mid turn geometry that ensures a consistent grip of the skis, which drives their turning action and provides us with a predictable platform to balance on.

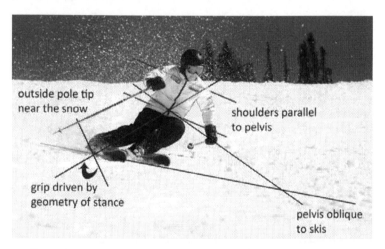

outside pole tip
near the snow

shoulders parallel
to pelvis

grip driven by
geometry of stance

pelvis oblique
to skis

Figure 15. Effective geometry at mid turn. The closer that simply balancing in a robust weight-bearing stance tilts our skis so they grip and perform the turn we intend, the closer we are to skiing well simply.

How to Balance During the Turn

1) Where to look. At mid turn, watching for the direction we want to be traveling in when exiting the turn helps us time our movements for releasing from the turn. Secondarily, looking to see what we will engage at the start of the subsequent turn helps to decide on any adjustments to our plan, possibly releasing earlier or later in order to have a little extra fun with a terrain feature, or to avoid something that wouldn't be fun at all.

2) What effort or movement to make. Balance is the guiding focus during the turn. Movements include turning the legs while the skis change direction, so the legs and feet change direction sooner than and more than the pelvis, and progressively bending forward at the hip joints. Efforts include keeping the upper body upright in the lateral direction so the tip of the outside pole hovers near the snow, and maintaining a resistive column of support comprising plantar tension, a strong outside leg, and just enough tension in the powerhouse to maintain posture.

3) What to feel. Seek to feel a steady and unmoving center of pressure on the sole of the outside foot, and, on average, equal pressure from both boot cuffs against shins and calves. Sensations from our boots provide biofeedback and help us achieve steady centered balance throughout the turn. With better balance, it is easier to relax the upper body and arms, tensing only enough to maintain posture amid the induced weight of the turn.

Balance is the crux of skiing. Good balance leads to good things, whereas poor balance leads to inefficient movement and wasted effort, wild recoveries, and entertaining replays of falls and crashes during après ski. Excellent balance is essential to ski well simply, and draws on what we see, how we stand, the efforts we make, and what we feel as a result.

Perfect Outcome at Mid Turn

At mid turn, our skis are gripping and performing the turn as we predicted, without any surprises. We feel our center of pressure steady on the arch side of the outside foot, and a smooth building of underfoot pressure as the turn progresses. We have no excess tension; no grimacing, no clenching of the jaw, no white-knuckled squeezing of the poles, no latched up muscles that inhibit our freedom to move. Skiing seems unrushed and flowing; we have time to scan ahead for where we want to ski.

For contrast, Figure 16 depicts problematic, ineffective stances for mid to late in the turn.

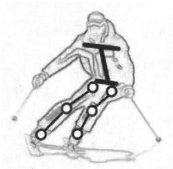 

Weak stance: too much leg turn
and forward bend at hip joint

Poor grip stance: upper body
square to the feet and skis

Figure 16. Common faults in stances during the turn. Our stance should evolve progressively with the turn in a manner that allows us to tilt our skis so they grip and turn, while keeping our skeletal frame such that we can expend the minimum effort to resist the induced weight of the turn.

Progression of Alignment, Geometry and Balance After Mid Turn

From mid turn through release from the turn, our alignment and geometry evolve while we balance on a steady center of pressure; the amount of pressure may vary but where on the soles of our feet we feel pressure remains steady. Success with keeping our center of pressure steady throughout the turn leads to increasing forward bend at the hip joints, and a perception that towards the end of the turn the feet and especially the outside foot moves ahead relative to the upper body. This easing ahead of the feet relative to the upper body is consistent with achieving a steady center of pressure, whether we sense deeper flex at the hip joints or the actually shift the feet ahead a little. Whatever our awareness or effort, forward flex in the hip joints increases towards the end of the turn when we pursue a steady center of pressure.

Happily, deeper flex in the hip joints contributes to effective Coiling, which ultimately leads to a smooth flow into the next turn. Alignment and Balance contribute to the skis gripping and turning effectively through mid turn, and Balance through the end of the turn leads to the third guiding focus in the Ski Well Simply model: Coiling.

COILING

<u>What is Coiling?</u>

Alignment and balance enable skiing groomed runs with relative ease, even with style and flair. But for versatility and maximum fun on steeper slopes and off piste terrain, we need more. This is where coiling comes in. What is coiling, and how does it contribute to skiing well simply? Coiling involves building torsion in the body during a turn and through release from the turn, then after release, letting that torsion help us align for the next turn.

Coiling is a game changer. I use coiling in every scenario; powder, moguls, gentle slow turns, hard fast carving turns, and even deep wet weather schmoo, the knee-deep gooey stuff that looks like, but isn't, powder. Coiling is especially helpful in tight quarters, moguls, trees and narrow chutes, and makes cruising and high speed skiing smoother and more reliable turn to turn. When I coil with precision, skiing becomes simpler, easier and more enjoyable. Without a doubt, coiling helps me to ski well simply.

Figure 17 depicts top views of the skis and direction of the pelvis when fully coiled.

<u>How to Coil</u>

Coiling is essentially achieved by turning our legs more than our upper body during each turn. Turning the legs means pointing the knees left or right of where the pelvis or belly button laser beam points. This is most easily accomplished by remaining balanced and following the changing direction of the skis by turning our legs without turning our upper body. The demarcation between upper and lower body being the hip joints, this means that nearly all rotary movement occurs in the hip joints; the legs turn while the skis change direction, resulting in a torsion in the body centered at the hip joints.

Staying centered and moving within stance geometries that allow us to resist the induced weight of the turn with a minimum of effort leads to notable obliqueness between skis and pelvis by the end of the turn. That obliqueness leads to a low effort transition to the next turn, since the skis carry the feet across under the upper body upon release from the turn to where we again align and balance going into the next turn.

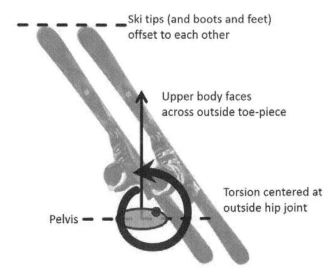

Figure 17. Coiled torsion builds in the powerhouse, centered at the hip joints, as the upper legs turn relative to the pelvis to accommodate the changing direction of the skis. By the point of release from the turn, there should be a noticeable obliqueness between the direction of the pelvis and the direction of the knees and skis.

Coiling and the buildup of torsion in the body is assisted by maintaining a steady fore-aft center of pressure from mid to late in the turn. Doing so requires increasing the amount of forward bend in the hip joints, in effect sliding the outside foot forward relative to the upper body. That increase in forward bend with the legs turned in the hip joint increases the amount of coiled torsion in the body, which upon release from the turn, assists in realigning the body going into the next turn. Coiling is also assisted by turn-induced loading. In fast sharp turns with noticeable peaks in loading, higher tensions in the body for resisting heavier induced weights lead to correspondingly stronger and faster-acting uncoiling forces between turns.

When turn-driven loading is subtle, such as when skiing slowly or gently, building enough torsion to contribute to the smooth linking of turns may require conscious effort or attention, say, to the relative directions of skis and upper body, or to feeling sensations in the body that signal torsion is present. While extra effort to coil may seem inefficient, making that effort helps to ingrain coiling into our skiing so it becomes automatic and helpful in all skiing situations. Happily, any such attention and effort provides instant gratification from a smooth and seemingly effortless flow to the next turn. Back to the particulars of coiling:

1) Where to look. Visualize where your belly button laser beam is shining as you approach where you will release from the turn. In long turns, it should shine close to the tip of the outside ski, and in short turns or slow gentle turns, across the toe-piece of the outside ski. Trace the specific line that you want your skis to travel during the next turn, and judge where you will be viewing from (where your head/eyes will be) by the time your skis begin to grip and curve your line of travel again. Having a specific objective in mind for the next turn guides your movements so your release from the turn leads to an alignment that targets a desired line of travel during the next turn.

2) What efforts and movements to make. Release begins by letting momentum take the upper body (and head) towards where you plan to be at the start of the next turn, while at the same time holding the skis tilted long enough to ensure they will carry the feet across and under the flight path of your upper body. This requires a conscious holding of the legs turned under the pelvis while letting momentum begin to take the upper body across and over the feet. It often requires, especially at higher speeds and pressures, a conscious shortening in stance—pulling the sternum forward, flexing deeper at the hips and knees—in order to remain centered and temporarily light in weight midway between turns. From mid transition, the goal is to flow into the next turn using a minimum of conscious effort. Relaxing as soon as and as much as possible allows momentum and the uncoiling of torsion in the body to contribute freely to alignment and preparation for the next turn. Executed perfectly, full relaxation after mid transition yields an alignment suited to the objectives of the next turn with near zero apparent effort. Full relaxation is a conceptual target; usually a little tension, a solid pole plant, or some other effort will be called for, but the goal is to flow smoothly into a balanced, relaxed, aligned stance, patiently awaiting the skis to begin the next turn, with a minimum of mindful effort.

3) What to feel. Expect to feel tension in leg and core muscles at the end of the turn and through release from the turn, especially when flexing to a shorter stance early in the transition to accommodate the feet being carried across and under the upper body. After mid transition, you may feel the upper legs turning back to neutral, square to the pelvis, as you relax the tension that was needed to resist the weight of the turn. The more you relax the more it seems like the body is acting automatically and without effort. As weight begins to rebuild, feeling weight on the outside foot centered, with the 'whole foot' engaged ball through heel on the arch side of the boot will affirm your preparedness for the next turn.

Our goal is to build coiled torsion to a maximum just before release from the turn, then to preserve that torsion through release to mid transition. Preserving torsion while releasing from the turn ensures that all the torsion accumulated during one turn contributes helpful torque to help our flow into the next turn. Between turns is 'payback time' with regards to coiling. Coiling (and uncoiling) is the primary focus at this stage of the turn cycle, as depicted in Figure 18.

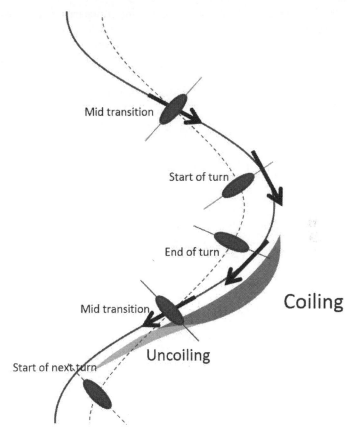

Figure 18. Coiling and its corollary, uncoiling, as a focus late in the turn and into the transition help guide efforts to achieve a free flowing progression from one turn to the next, using minimum effort.

Cues for Twist (be twisted, and happier for it)

What are some cues that can help to coil? After all, it is difficult to sense what the pelvis is doing and where it is pointed. We can feel things moving but are unable to gauge with any real precision how much they are moving.

My favorite external cue is the belly button laser beam because it offers precision and encourages symmetry whether turning left or right. From earlier, the direction that the laser beam shines in is the direction that your pelvis faces in. By mid turn and definitely by the exit from the turn, your skis should have turned to where the laser beam shines across your outside ski, confirming obliqueness between skis and pelvis. If the skis point at the twelve o'clock, then by the end of a turn the laser beam should shine downhill of that by a few minutes, perhaps three to eight minutes, depending on the situation. See Figure 19.

Figure 19. Top view depicting the direction of the upper body relative to the direction of the skis at release from the turn. The tighter the turn, the greater the difference between the direction of the skis and upper body, or more importantly, the direction of the legs and pelvis.

Yet another visual cue is seeing the tip of the inside ski resting ahead of the tip of the outside ski at mid turn, which is the desired result of turning the legs without turning the pelvis. The pelvis in line with the offset of the tips makes it easy to bend forward at the hip joints in the direction that momentum is willing you to travel, or, to grab an imagined box of apples (or case of wine) as described earlier in BALANCE. It may help to picture an elastic band stretched between the ski tips, and keep your pelvis parallel to that elastic. Think 'angle of the tips is the angle of the hips' or succinctly, 'tips to hips', so your pelvis faces across your outside ski while the skis turn, and down the hill late in the turn (see Figure 17 again).

Regarding sensations, when coiled, standing with the upper legs turned to the inside of the turn and resisting the induced weight of the turn, you should feel tension that is linked to rotational and forward flexion in the hip joints. How this feels will vary from person to person, and may feel differently for a turn to the left versus a turn to the right, especially for bodies that are asymmetric in flexibility or strength. Even a minor asymmetry in flexibility can lead to asymmetry in stance geometry for a turn to the left versus right, especially if we rely strictly on how coiling feels. I often see skiers appearing less flexible on their stronger side, and introducing an asymmetry to their stance, turns, and the reliability of the turning action from their skis. Practicing with a specific external cue, such as the belly button laser shining across the outside toe-piece late in the turn, encourages precise symmetrical movements.

Another important cue for effective coiling relates to bending forward at the hip joints. Some forward bend at the hip joints primes stabilizing muscles in the powerhouse for balancing purposes, and facilitates a larger range of lateral and rotational flex in the hip joints for coiling purposes. What can help pursue enough forward bend through the end of the turn? Late in the turn and into the early part of the transition, I imagine 'wringing' out' the old turn by consciously holding my legs turned while I flex forward at the hip joints, pulling my sternum in the direction of my belly button laser, as if my whole body is a wet cloth that I want to wring the water out of as I exit the turn. This imagery and effort helps prevent suddenly squaring my pelvis to the direction of my skis while I release from the turn, and thus erasing any torsion that would have helped me align for the next turn. Core tension until my upper body passes across my skis also helps to ensure that my skis don't jet ahead of me while I exit the turn.

A final note on twist: too much of a good thing can definitely be a bad thing. Too much offset in the direction of pelvis versus knees and skis reduces our strength and mobility. It also leaves the torso facing partially sideways to its momentum and the upcoming 'action', less than ideal for dealing with balance challenges going into the next turn. Too much offset also risks discomfort and pain. There's no need to overdo or force the amount of twist, all that is needed is enough to create some torque that will help realign our bodies between turns.

<u>Release and Relax</u>

Release from the turn means letting momentum dictate our line of travel from one turn to the next. During the turn, we resist the weight that accompanies the turn so that our line of travel curves. During release, we allow momentum to take our upper body across our skis towards the inside of the next turn, and our skis and feet across and under our upper body. There are two key objectives for a good release: preserve ski-to-pelvis obliqueness and coiled torsion until mid-transition, and, manage pressure in the early part of the transition in order to be light in weight but still in contact with the snow long enough to align and prepare for the next turn before weight increases again. A light or reduced weight interval is best for allowing uncoiling torsion to help align for the next turn, long enough time-wise to allow a brief relaxation between turns. Even a minor reduction in weight allows any torsion that was preserved while releasing from the turn to contribute.

At release from the turn, which is when we reduce or cease resisting the loading of the turn and let momentum take our upper body, is a critical instant. Our skis, being oblique to the direction that momentum pulls us, bring the feet from out to one side to directly under us at mid transition. If during this time we keep our outside leg the same length, or, don't bend the knee any more than it is already, we will experience an upwards thrust that pushes us up and away from the slope. Our options during this instant from release to mid transition are to decrease, hold or add to whatever upwards boost we experience in order to achieve a time interval of reduced weight that lasts long enough for us to align and prepare for the next turn before the skis start curving our line of travel again, and before our weight starts increasing again. Figure 20 provides a pictorial of the transition from one turn to the next.

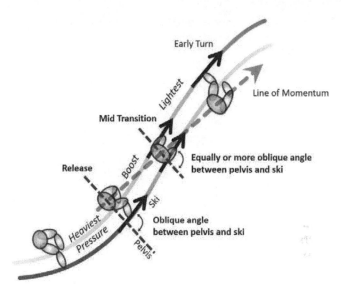

Figure 20. Release through transition. Reducing resistance to the loading of the turn while holding the skis sufficiently tilted so they carry the feet across and under the upper body drives the switch from one turn to the next. Lessening the strength with which we resist underfoot pressure allows momentum to carry the upper body towards the inside of the next turn. Preserving the obliqueness of skis and upper body and thus torsion in the powerhouse during release leads to a least effort preparation for the next turn.

To the extent that we shorten or extend our stance while exiting the turn, or, reduce or add pressure during release, we can affect the amount of upwards boost we feel as we exit the turn. The ideal amount for the simplest skiing is just enough that we become near weightless but with our skis still in contact with the snow. The length of time that we remain light is related to our speed. The faster the speed, the longer the time it is possible to be light; essentially, we are flying low. This effect is muted at slow speeds. At slow speeds, a drop in weight can be subtle and elusive to feel, but even a brief reduction in pressure allows the tension gained by coiling to benefit our flow into the next turn. Figure 21 describes the boost effect that often occurs after letting momentum define the flow of our upper body and skis between turns.

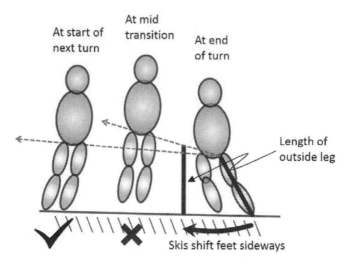

At start of
next turn

At mid
transition

At end
of turn

Length of
outside leg

Skis shift feet sideways

Figure 21. Holding the outside leg at a fixed bend or extending it at release will boost the body upwards and away from the slope. To retain contact with the snow (and not fly too far between turns) requires adjusting body tension so that the feet can move freely across under the upper body. This effect and the movements we make to manage it are somewhat proportional to speed and the quicker the skis take the feet across under the body between turns; at times, an active retraction of the feet upwards towards the chest is necessary to maintain contact with the snow.

The light feeling after release gives the opportunity to relax and fully benefit from coiling. Relaxing allows the torsion to uncoil our body and contribute our preparations for the next turn. The goal is to use no more tension or effort than required to prepare for the upcoming turn. The better our execution, the more we can relax and feel like our alignment is automatic and effortless. Relaxation requires conscious attention to relaxing, being patient, and letting things develop naturally. If we interfere by staying too tense or by doing more than necessary (such as trying to turn rather than just balance), we reduce the benefits of coiling and make our skiing more complex and more work than it needs to be.

My preferred release move is to let momentum take my upper body while I flex in the hip joints, with effort ranging from just relaxing my legs a little to actively retracting as if to lift my skis off the snow. Such movement is a continuum of flexing at the hip joints aimed at maintaining a steady fore-aft center of pressure throughout the turn, or absorbing the burst of pressure from a mogul at the end of a turn. Flexing also allows my feet to cross under my upper body without it getting pushed up and away from the slope so quickly that I get popped off the snow (more than I may have intended). My usual goal is to experience some lightness in weight between turns, but to stay in contact with the snow. Lightness allows me to relax and enjoy the benefits of coiling, but too much means that I'm airborne and fully at the mercy of momentum. Having said that, at times I actually want to be airborne, for a bit of fun with a terrain feature, or possibly to skip a dip between two moguls, rather than pound into a nasty-looking trough. Getting airborne may call for extending my legs at release, an easy choice given my flexed stance late in the turn. Generally though, I seek to maintain contact with the snow between turns, so relax or retract my feet actively enough to achieve a lightweight contact at mid transition. The faster the switch occurs, as driven by my speed and the amount of obliqueness between my skis and pelvis at release, the more actively I need to retract my feet upwards in order to stay in contact with the snow.

Figure 22 shows a typical release from one turn through alignment and entry to the next turn. The rightmost image is just at the point of release, where my upper body is being taken by momentum while I keep my skis tilted to ensure that their momentum carries my feet across and under me; here, a slight flex in the knee allows my feet to begin crossing under my upper body without popping me off the snow. The middle image is where I am light in weight, skis barely touching the snow, while momentum continues to carry my feet across under my upper body. Being light I can easily extend my legs, in particular my new outside leg, so it is ready for an increase in weight during the upcoming turn. The leftmost image is just as the turn starts. Here my outside leg is extended and ready for an increase in weight, my feet are on the magic carpet, and I am seeking to feel pressure centered along the arch side of my outside foot, using plantar tension to ensure that I am on the foot, the whole foot, and nothing but the foot.

Figure 22. Between turns, momentum and the release of coiled torsion help to reorient and align the body for the next turn. Momentum reorients the body when there is an oblique angle between the direction of the pelvis and skis at release from the turn, so the momentum of the skis carry the feet across under the upper body while the momentum of the upper body propels it along its line of travel. Simultaneously, relaxing enables coiled torsion to contribute freely to turning the legs from oblique to square relative to the pelvis, contributing to a relaxed readiness for the new turn.

Letting momentum take us wherever it may is not as scary as it sounds. During the turn, our upper body faces towards the outside of the turn, and at any instant, towards where we expect momentum to carry us whenever we choose to release from the turn. The upper body facing the direction that momentum will carry us between turns means that whenever we release and let momentum take over, we will be facing squarely towards the immediate upcoming 'action' that awaits us. Facing the action ensures that we are best positioned to deal with whatever is imminent.

Consequences of Not Preserving Twist During Release

Letting momentum and uncoiling torque rule between turns is key to effortless linking of turns, and preserving torsion through the release allows the simplest possible skiing. The flipside is avoiding doing anything that prevents the accumulated and preserved torsion from contributing freely. If we tense too much or move in a manner than interferes with its contribution, we add complexity and inefficiency in our skiing.

For example, if we anticipate our skis turning, and swing our upper body into that direction in order to 'help' them turn, we actually reduce how effectively the skis grip and turn. We do unnecessary work and get less from our skis in return, which makes us do yet more work! Here's why. Turning our upper body into the direction of the turn eliminates the geometrically-driven ski tilt that we enjoy with the pelvis oblique to the skis and a forward bend at the hip joints. The resulting loss in grip spurs us to do something to make the skis turn; probably a sustained effort to turn the shoulders into the turn. I'm sure you've seen skiers with their shoulders twisted into the turn, their outside arm across their body, and their downhill pole pointing precariously ahead and ready to vault them skyward should it ever catch the snow. Rotating the upper body in the direction of the turn in advance of the turning action of the skis also negates coiling, which means no torque to help us flow from one turn to the next.

Another common foible, squaring the pelvis to the direction of the skis at the end of the turn, is easy to do when releasing from the turn. Squaring as such leaves the upper body facing too much towards the outside of the new turn and partially sideways to where momentum is pulling us. A common reaction is then to rotate the upper body into the direction of the new turn which, as just explained, reduces the tilt and grip of the skis and leads to us doing more than simply balance during the turn. Such corrective movements take effort and disrupt flow, a self-perpetuated self-defeating loop. Leaving the direction of the pelvis unchanged and unfettered while exiting the turn is worth every bit of attention that we can muster. In summary, we want to be skilled at flexing and extending at the hip joints while standing with both legs turned to the left or right relative to the pelvis.

Try this. Stand facing a wall. Turn both feet to a forty-five degree angle to the wall, but keep your pelvis and belly button facing squarely at the wall. Place your hands on your hips. Now flex and straighten a few times between a half squat and standing straight. While doing so, look down to see if your pelvis changes direction at all. It shouldn't if you are able to flex vertically without turning your upper body, especially when your legs are equally oblique to your pelvis. Between one turn and the next our skis roll through flat on the snow while having minimal pressure on them, so they are free to be influenced by whatever our legs do between turns. If you are unable to crouch without rotating the pelvis while standing on a high-friction floor, it is likely that you will have a hard time realizing the full benefits of coiling when standing on a pair of slippery skis. Here's something interesting: try flexing between a half squat and tall stance without changing the bend in your ankles, which simulates what happens in stiff ski boots. A constant forward bend at the ankles, as encouraged by our ski boots, leads to flexing mostly in the hip joints, and very little in the knees (they stay bent at a steady angle, so aren't flexing much). Is it easier now to keep the pelvis from turning when you flex and extend? Aha! Squatting, or bending the knees as we would do in order to sit on a chair is to be avoided. Doing so makes it harder to retain obliqueness between skis and pelvis, which tends to flatten the skis and compromise their grip, and reduces the amount of coiled torsion in the body that would otherwise assist our flow from one turn to the next.

Figure 23 shows my actions through release, tracking images from late in the turn through mid transition. During this interval, I flex and extend at the hip joints without affecting the direction of my pelvis. Note that flexing of the outside knee to accommodate my feet crossing under my upper body occurs only after my switch is well underway. After mid transition, aligning and balancing in preparation for the next turn takes very little effort since the uncoiling torque in my body continues to help me align while my skis carry my feet across under my upper body.

Perfect Outcome from Effective Coiling

Extending while relaxing after release from the turn leads to flowing into the next turn with our alignment and stance geometry exactly suiting the objectives of that turn.

What Happens Next

Next in the turn cycle comes alignment. The key here is to let the torsion accumulated by coiling do its work. Torque from uncoiling turns the legs from oblique to the pelvis at end of turn to straight ahead, helping align our stance for the next turn, while weight centered on the arch side of the outside foot encourages the skis to grip and start the next turn. From there, continued turning of the feet and legs in sync with the turning action of the skis develops obliqueness between the pelvis and skis by mid turn, and continued flexing forward at the hip joint in order to retain a steady center of pressure leads to full coiling by the end of the turn.

Figure 23. Release from the turn. I often pretend to 'wring out' the old turn as a way to 'bring in' the new. 'Wringing out' or hinging more deeply at the hip joints while releasing (images 2 and 3) helps me preserve torsion accumulated during the turn, and keeps my skis tilted so they carry my feet across under my upper body. It also keeps my upper body from getting left behind while I exit the turn, so I don't get caught back on my heels going into the new turn. At mid transition, my skis are still oblique to my upper body (image 4). From there, uncoiling torsion springs my legs back towards neutral while weight centered on the arch side of the outside foot coaxes my skis to grip and begin the next turn.

Alignment should be a patient process, but it is possible to hurry it up when necessary. With pent up torsion present, pulling ourselves back into alignment takes less effort. Sometimes our balance or orientation is out of sorts and the upcoming terrain demands a quick adjustment. Between turns offers a brief window of lightness and straight travel in which to get ourselves reorganized. Truncating a turn, releasing early, is a tactic to help regain form without losing turn-to-turn rhythm. Here, obliqueness at mid turn can be converted into helpful torque; 'fix it in the air' is an option that comes to mind. It may not be pretty, but it can suffice to preserve rhythm and flow.

BLENDING

While breaking down skiing into specific focuses is helpful for understanding, eye-pleasing flowing skiing requires blending what we see, do and feel. So far, I've discussed three primary focuses to guide our movements, but what about the timing of those movements? What focus can help us link our movements and efforts in pursuit of alignment, balancing and coiling so our skiing becomes as much fun to do as it is inspiring to watch?

I believe that focus is related to the rise and fall in the pressure we experience up through our feet as our skis serpentine our line of travel down the mountain. Physics dictates that each turn or change in direction that our skis deliver induces an increase in pressure up through our feet, as depicted in Figure 24. Moving in a manner that amplifies the changes in underfoot pressure, while keeping those changes smooth, helps to blend align, balance and coil into effective flowing skiing.

Figure 24. Pressure ebb and flow for a typical series of linked turns. The solid line represents the line traveled by our skis, and the shading shows a desirable underfoot pressure cycle. Underfoot pressure increases with each turn due to forces that act sideways to our instantaneous momentum or instantaneous direction of travel. Best results achieve smooth changes in pressure, increasing from lightest pressure after mid transition to heaviest pressure just before release from the turn.

It's A Pressure Skiing This Way

How do we 'feel' underfoot pressure so we can use it as feedback? Skiing at higher speeds can mean pressures during the turn heavy enough to buckle a weak posture; at lower speeds the rise and fall in underfoot pressure can be very subtle and hard to feel. With this wide range of possible pressures, I prefer to focus on the soles of my feet, since I am already attuned to how my boots feel for balancing purposes.

Other indicators are how much tension I need in the powerhouse or how much effort it takes to hold my arms steady under the loading of the turn. Whatever you choose, find something and tune into it. You'll benefit by being encouraged to move with each turn, and to move in time with each turn.

What movements will amplify underfoot pressure and improve our timing and blending of movements. We can increase the pressure on our feet in two basic ways. The preferred way is to flex progressively and mainly at the hip joint en route to the sharpest and heaviest point in the turn, then to ease out of that heaviest feeling while releasing from the turn. Where the skis change direction the fastest will be where pressure is greatest, and where we are coiled and ready to release from the turn. In this movement pattern, flexing occurs mainly at the hip joint, with very little flexing at the knee (changing the amount of bend at the knee) until releasing from the turn.

A secondary means is flexing or extending vertically in order to temporarily reduce or increase underfoot pressure. For example, when we encounter a mogul, we can flex to absorb, or reduce, the pressure we would experience if we were to brace, stiff and unyielding. Generating pressure changes through vertical flexing also has its place in soft powder in order to coax the skis to mimic a springboard or trampoline. Punching the skis downward during a turn, then enjoying their rebound upwards where they readily move across and under the body so as to produce the next turn when they sink into the snow again. This movement pattern involves flexing at both the hip joints and knees. Note that in either of these two movement patterns, the forward angle in the ankle remains virtually unchanged: by doing so we maintain equal pressure on the shin and calf of the boot cuff, and more readily remain centered on 'the foot, whole foot, and nothing but the foot'.

Our movements can be performed quickly, or slowly, depending on the dynamics of a particular instant. Whatever the situation, our skiing becomes simpler when pressure changes, whether increasing or decreasing, occur smoothly. Trying to 'pressure the skis' by thrusting down with the legs can be wasteful and disruptive; better to sense the pressure the skis deliver turn to turn and time our movements, flexing at the hip joints, or at both the hip joints and knees, to amplify the underfoot pressure ever so slightly. Judiciously reducing our resistance to underfoot pressure can minimize banging or jarring from underfoot, especially when the terrain is rough and variable, and steady our view of the upcoming terrain. Better vision, better anticipation, better result: keep it smooth becomes the mantra.

Figure 25 shows some undesirable pressure patterns during turns. Sudden peaks in pressure can occur when the skis are swiveled and edged in a typical 'slow me down now!' fear-inspired instant. Smoother results are more likely attained the skis are allowed to determine the turn based on us remaining balanced and centered while they change direction. Even where the skis are making the turn, we can lapse into placid unexciting skiing if we stand passively, rather than move in order to earn a little extra swell in underfoot pressure.

Figure 25. Depiction of less-than-optimal pressure patterns with each turn. Sudden changes in pressure or no change in pressure is suboptimal for pursuing and achieving smooth flowing skiing.

The bottom line: pursuing smooth increases and decreases in underfoot pressure, in rhythm with the turns that our skis produce, helps us blend our movements and efforts for a delightful skiing experience.

Maximize Mileage, Repeat, Repeat, Repeat

Blending to an expert level takes time, distance, and lots of turns. Because ski time is precious, I prefer to hone my skills within skiing, focusing on a given movement or effort with each turn, such as emphasizing a movement or zeroing in on a specific sensation at a selected point in each turn. At times I alternate between a series of turns in which I exaggerate the movements or efforts related to a chosen focus, then a series of regular turns to see if I can sense the desired improvement. When something is proving elusive either in my execution or in my sensing and feeling of what I expect, my last resort is to take a few minutes and work a specific drill to explore that hard-to-get element.

I usually work one focus on any given day, for example, feeling my center of pressure in the perfect spot on the sole of my outside foot throughout every turn, or, ensuring that my belly button laser beam shines exactly across the toe-piece of my outside ski at the end of every turn, or, how well my movements create a smooth rise and fall in pressure with each turn. I seek precision and consistency with whatever focus I've chosen and ski a variety of steepnesses and snow conditions, working my focus du jour with each turn. Choosing a particular focus and skiing different situations with that focus at the top of my attention checklist allows me to incorporate skill building within skiing, and keep time spent drilling for skills to a minimum.

Before looking at some self-training ideas, let's review the overall flow from turn to turn. Often, stating something a little differently boosts understanding, and helps to blend in our minds what we seek to blend on the hill.

Review of the Overall Process

Alignment, balance and coiling repeat as leading focuses during the turn-to-turn cycle, albeit they overlap and morph from one to the next. Here's a quick review of how I use Align-Balance-Coil to ski well simply.

Alignment targets flowing into the turn in an extended stance with a good portion of weight concentrated along the arch of the new outside foot. A quality release from the previous turn produces a lightweight that makes it easy to extend before the weight of the new turn arrives. I resist the urge to do anything to speed up the start of the next turn, such as turning my legs into the turn or flexing my stance in some manner; instead I patiently let the skis start to shape the turn. I use plantar tension to fully engage the sole of my outside foot, feeling weight on the ball through the heel. I hold my arms extended symmetrically out to the front and sides, and keep my upper body upright in the lateral direction so the tip of my outside pole hovers just above the snow.

Balance is my guiding focus during the turn, my goal being a steady center of pressure on my outside foot such that ball through heel of that foot remains fully engaged throughout the turn. Success finds me able to resist the loading of the turn with a strong weight-bearing stance that evolves from extended and relaxed at the start of the turn to flexed, mainly at the hip joints, late in the turn. My mid turn geometry develops as a result of turning my legs to accommodate, and assist if necessary, the turning action of my skis, being sure that my skis change direction sooner than and more than my pelvis does. To promote keeping my center of pressure steady, I hold my feet parallel and within the magic carpet, use plantar tension under a strong outside leg, and just enough tension in my powerhouse to maintain my stance throughout the induced weight of the turn. I seek to feel underfoot pressure build smoothly and peak at the apex of the turn, more so the sharper the intended turn. A smooth increase in pressure encourages a smooth change in the geometry of my stance, and helps my skis grip consistently and reliably as the turn progresses. That consistent and reliable grip minimizes surprises and keeps my balancing act simple.

Coiling becomes the key focus late in the turn. My guiding thought is to ensure that my feet become sufficiently oblique to the direction of my pelvis and upper body by late in the turn, and then to not lose the torsion earned by coiling until after releasing from the turn. I build torsion in the powerhouse by exploiting the turning action of my skis, with just enough tension in the upper body to keep it aligned to itself. Having endured the maximum pressure of the turn with a strong grip-promoting stance, I begin my release by pulling my sternum across my skis in the direction along which I expect to 'fly low' between turns. I complete the release by flexing below the waist just enough that the pressure under my feet reduces. During release, I pay particular attention to not disturbing the direction of my pelvis. My upper body becomes purely cargo after release, no more than a passive contributor to momentum, yet available to be an active contributor if necessary to help me align and balance before entering the new turn.

My goal at release from the turn is to achieve lightness between turns so I can easily extend my overall stance before pressure starts building again in the new turn. Minimal pressure on my feet during the switch from one turn to the next allows momentum to dictate my line of travel and to carry my feet from one side of my upper body to the other. During the switch, my skis are relatively flat on the snow and lightly pressured, allowing me to prepare for the next turn with a minimum of effort, assisted by the uncoiling torque in my powerhouse.

A key goal during release is to have my upper body squarely facing the line of travel that momentum will 'fly' it along during the transition. I want my upper body facing along its direction of travel so that I am best prepared to deal with challenges that may arise where the next turn begins, such as an upcoming mogul or a deep rut in the snow, especially where my weight will increase in the new turn. Essentially I want to be 'facing the action', with my torso squarely facing any immediate challenges, akin to facing a tennis opponent who is about to unleash a monster serve, or, more pertinent to skiing, facing the induced loading that I'll need to resist as the next turn takes shape. I may need to use a pole plant just after I release in order to correct where my torso faces between turns, but if I am well balanced, a light touch of the pole is sufficient. Being attentive to a well-timed movement and light touch the pole with each turn, even when I could do without, is good practice to ensure that I am trained and ready to plant a pole firmly when needed.

While my body crosses over my feet and my feet cross under my body, I relax and extend to help my powerhouse uncoil, which unconsciously releases some torque and helps me align my posture for the next turn. Uncoiling turns my legs relative to my pelvis, turning them from where they pointed late in the last turn towards where they best suit the next turn. With perfect execution and snow conditions, uncoiling torsion contributes all the torque needed to align; I can simply relax until the turn takes hold. When the snow isn't quite as friendly, I can inject some tension or effort as necessary to align and balance going into the turn. Any effort for such fine-tuning is usually minimal, since the torque from uncoiling is already doing much of the work.

For best flow, I seek to avoid influencing the direction of my body and pelvis between turns. Any conscious turning of the upper body, and specifically, the pelvis, into the direction of the new turn reduces tilt and thus edge grip on my skis. This triggers instinctive reactions to recover the lost grip, and detracts from the simplicity of letting momentum and uncoiling do their work. I get the best outcomes when I relax out of the torsion that was built from coiling in one turn and extend into an aligned stance that suits my intentions for the upcoming turn. The closer I am to having momentum and uncoiling alone help me flow into an alignment that ultimately leads to the turn shape and speed I intend, the closer I am to skiing well simply.

Coiling is simplest when the skis grip the snow sufficiently to change direction while we do no more than balance on them. Our body coils and develops torsion to the extent that we keep the pelvis from changing direction as much as the legs and skis do while the skis perform the turn. When the skis offer little in the way of pressure or turning action, building coiled tension in the body takes conscious effort to have our legs and skis become sufficiently oblique to the direction of our pelvis and upper body. It is possible to actively twist our bodies into torsion, such as by counter-rotating or turning our upper body towards the outside of the turn, or rotating our upper body into the turn to encourage the skis to change direction, but to ski simply we want the turning action of our skis to guide our movements that in turn build torsion. A corollary source of assistance for coiling is the loading of the turn. That loading results from an effective alignment which ensures ski grip, which leads to increasing underfoot pressure and induced weight. The increased weight works to compress our stance to the extent that we allow, the best choice being to flex mainly at the hip joints, so the legs and in particular the outside leg, can remain 'long and strong' to help resist the induced weight of the turn. Deepening the flex in the hip joints allows more rotational freedom for coiling, and facilitates building torsion with minimal stress to the spine and back.

To summarize, coiling should build with minimal effort, assisted by the loading of the turn and the turning action of the skis. Release is triggered by a movement that gives the upper body up to momentum, immediately followed by less pressure on the feet to allow a smooth switch while the feet traverse under the upper body between turns. Less weight underfoot allows momentum to rule, dictating the lines of travel of both the upper body and the feet. Between turns, relaxing and letting momentum and uncoiling torsion help to realign for the next turn feels pleasingly effortless and contributes to smooth flow into the next turn. This continuum of action and outcome is a blending of movements and efforts into a flow that is pleasing to watch and even more pleasing to experience.

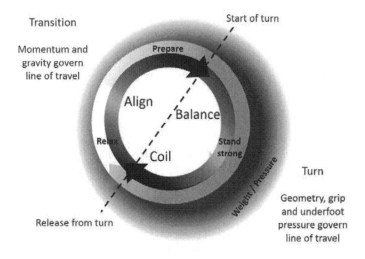

Figure 26. Align-Balance-Coil cycle revisited, showing the interplay and overlap of alignment, balancing, and coiling, and the rise and fall in underfoot pressure. Balance envelops the cycle, overlapping with Alignment to drive turning action of the skis, which leads to Coiling, which then leads to assisted Alignment for the next turn, repeating ad infinitum.

Specific Focuses Within the Align-Balance-Coil Cycle

To keep things simple when skiing, it helps to target precise goals, and work to achieve those goals with each turn. I recommend selecting one daily goal and working with it. Pursuing a specific cue or outcome, and correcting as necessary in order to achieve that cue or outcome with every turn is a proven way to ingrain new movement patterns.

I have a handful of specific goals that I work with from time to time in order to keep my skiing tuned. I prefer to work on these in bursts, rather than continuously throughout the day. I find it best to work with these early in the day or just after lunch, once I have made enough turns to be warmed up and ready to focus on particulars. On many days, just skiing is the objective, feeling the flow. On these days, I may occasionally zero in on a particular thought for a few turns to check my precision against a selected cue or outcome. I rarely choose more than one focus within a given day. One focus at a time is enough. I shudder when I hear someone rhyming off a whole raft of thoughts that they have floating around in their heads. How they can possibly ski with all that tumbling around in their head, the operative word being tumbling, escapes me.

Advice: choose one focus, and work with only that one focus. Take comfort that focusing on any single topic will ripple through the whole process, improving other aspects of your skiing at the same time. Trying to focus on more than one thing at a time is asking for confusion about what you are seeking to do or feel. When we have a strong desire to improve, narrowing to one focus and striving for success with that focus is likely to yield progress and satisfaction. Conversely, a scattered approach, or a lack of persistence, usually yields little reward and ongoing frustration.

Here are some specific focuses that I use in my skiing, as examples:

1) Steady and unchanging center of pressure on the outside foot throughout each turn. This one is easy to isolate with any type of turn and at any speed. Use plantar tension to modulate the pressure on the ball and heel of the outside foot before the turn begins. On firmer snow, add some effort to roll the foot so that weight concentrates along the arch side of the outside foot, and seek to feel pressure steady and centered on the sole of the outside foot throughout the turn. Don't worry about the

amount of pressure on the inside foot, but do keep your knees as far apart as your skis. Knees as far apart as the skis will keep both skis performing similarly and thus produce fewer surprises.

2) Belly button facing across the outside toe piece at the end of the turn, especially in moguls and short or slow turns. During long open cruising turns, seek to have the belly button aim closer to the tip of the outside ski. At the end of the turn, you should feel tension somewhere in the powerhouse, which tells you that torsion is available to help you realign for the next turn.

3) Zero turning of the pelvis during release from the turn. Tip: during release, pull the sternum forward in the direction it will travel en route to the start of the next turn, and allow momentum to take your upper body in that direction before letting go of the tilt on your skis. I find it helpful to imagine 'wringing out' the old turn, as if my body were a wet cloth that I want to wring the water out of. These elements help from exiting the turn with the weight too far back.

4) Zero turning of the pelvis early in the turn. Exercise idea: while entering the new turn, place your outside hand (or knuckles) on the corresponding outside front corner of your pelvic bone. As the turn develops, seek to have your pelvis not change direction, at all, until the turning of your skis necessitates the pelvis follow them while they change direction. Keep working this focus until you feel zero turning of the pelvis ahead of when the turning action of the skis causes your upper body to change direction. Remember: the skis turn sooner than and more than the pelvis does.

5) After releasing from the turn, do nothing except balance and wait for the skis to start the next turn. If you have coiled sufficiently, the next turn will indeed start. Let the unwinding torsion in your body contribute freely; seek minimum effort while feeling your weight centered along the arch side of your outside foot, rolling the foot slightly inside your boot to accentuate the sensation. It may take a while before the skis start the turn, especially if the previous turn ended with insufficient obliqueness or torsion, or if you are doing something that interferes with the release of pent up torque. Choose an easy groomed run and be sure that you have enough space in case your new turn takes a while to start. As you get better at coiling, the distance between turns will become quite short. Try it!

Typical Issues and Corrective Suggestions

At times, there are focuses or objectives that we all struggle with. What should we do when things 'go wrong', or less well than we would like? This section summarizes some common difficulties and recommends related drills or focuses that can help address the issue, followed by a list of drills to develop movement patterns that are pertinent to the Align-Balance-Coil model. Note that the drills are ordered roughly in sequence of difficulty, so use the lower numbers first and work up to the higher numbers for better success.

Issue: "I just can't stop the urge to turn my upper body to get the turn started. I'm worried that if I don't do that, I'll get going too fast before my skis turn." Recommendation: focus on alignment and balance, only; think 'balance', not 'turn'. Practice with drills 3, 5, 7, and 13.

Issue: "I often find myself falling over towards the inside of the turn." Again, balance to the rescue. Recommendation: seek to feel the outside foot, fully engaged ball through heel, and the center of pressure on its sole steady throughout the turn. Use plantar tension. Practice with drills 2, 6, and 8.

Issue: "Try as I may, I can't get my skis to grip the snow; they just slip sideways so much that I often spin out, and end up facing across the hill or feeling like Bambi lying with legs splayed on an icy pond." This one can be due to poorly aligned boots, such that when standing neutral and centered, the skis are tilted outwards. This leads to poor grip, or grip that can only be attained with awkward and weak postures. Recommendation: have a good boot fitter fix the boot issues, and do that now. Then, practice with drills 4, 6, 9, and 12.

Issue: "I keep getting caught with my weight back, struggling to stay upright. My calves repeatedly get hammered into the backs of my boot cuffs. Help!" This is a basic balance issue. This skier is falling backwards with each turn, possibly after getting away with standing on their heels early in the day when the snow was softer. Later in the day when the snow is firmer or bumpier, the problem emerges. The skis keep sliding ahead and the skier is repeatedly getting caught in the dreaded 'back seat'. Recommendation: learn what it feels like to be centered fore and aft. Practice with drills 1, 2, 4, 7, and 11.

Issue: "I don't get 'turning my legs', it just feels alien." It is hard to get the body to accept having the legs pointing in a different direction than the upper body, but it is worth learning for the benefits it produces, namely, better grip during the turn and an easier transition to the next turn. Recommendation: pursue standing and flexing while the legs are turned under the pelvis to get familiar with the related positions and sensations. Practice with drills 3, 4, 7, and 8.

Issue: "My switch between turns feels really awkward. I seem to be working way too hard to get from one turn to the next." Recommendation: pursue coiling and centered balance late in the turn. To get our body to cross over our feet while our feet cross under our body, we want to finish the turn with an oblique angle between the belly button laser and our skis. This obliqueness will then cause momentum to drive the switch in inclination of our body between turns. Practice with drills 1, 3, 5, 8, and 10.

<u>Drills for Blending Skills</u>

There are a handful of drills that I find quite fun to intersperse with regular skiing. I like these since they parallel what serves good skiing and are easy to ski in and out of. Using this tactic can help advance a particular skill more quickly than just skiing, yet not detract much from regular ski time.

1) Flex taller and smaller. When stopped on a flat area, stand with your feet parallel and on the magic carpet. Flex as deeply as possible and then stand tall again, without changing how your ski boots feel on your soles and against your shins and calves. Once you have this working when standing still, repeat a few times while skiing slowly along a very gentle slope (check that there's nobody around who might see you, or worse, video you doing this). Best results occur when you flex only in the hip joints and the knees, leaving the bend in the ankles constant as defined by your ski boots. Develops flexing and extending without disturbing or moving your center of pressure.

2) Play with plantar tension. Stand on the magic carpet and alternately press down and ease up on the amount of pressure on the balls of your feet. The effort is subtle, just enough to change the ratio of weight on the balls and heels of your feet but without lifting your heels. Try playing with different amounts of plantar tension while skiing on gentle groomed areas or along roads to familiarize with how to make the effort without losing balance, and to discover how your skis react to your efforts. After you have some familiarity with the effort and the result, experiment with adding plantar tension at different parts of the turn, say, early versus late in the turn. The results can be enlightening. Develops using plantar tension to adjust the center of pressure.

3) Single turn to a stop, with torsion assist. Stand with skis parallel and across the hill, and one or two boot widths apart. Slide your uphill ski forward a little and turn your upper body so your belly button aims across the toe-piece of the downhill ski. Bend forward a little at the hip joints, and check that you are centered on your feet, with equal pressure on shins and calves, and most weight on the downhill foot. Now look straight downhill to a spot on the snow about ten to fifteen feet away, and push yourself forward using your poles with an intention of doing one turn and stopping where you are looking. Your skis should turn quickly, seemingly automatically, due to the unwinding torsion in your powerhouse, bringing you to a stop facing in the opposite direction to what you started in. The

key is to be sure you are balanced and centered and that you let the skis turn, rather than try to force them to turn. Secondly, when you stop you should be standing with your upper body oblique to your skis so your belly button is again aimed across the toe-piece of your downhill ski. Try single turns and linked turns as such on groomed slopes that are rated green or blue. Excellent introduction to the effects of coiling. Develops relaxation and patience, and avoiding any turning of the upper body to invoke the start of a turn.

4) Slippery traverse. CAUTION: watch uphill so you don't interfere with other sliders and riders. Same stance as in drill #3, with the skis across the hill and the pelvis oblique to the skis, the belly button aimed near the downhill toe-piece. Slide in a straight line along the direction that your pelvis is faced in; near equally between straight across the hill and straight down the hill. Adjust the tilt on your skis so they slip slowly and steadily, likely by moving your knees sideways about an inch or so in the downhill direction. Keep your feet offset, with uphill foot ahead of downhill foot, so it is comfortable to keep the pelvis oblique the skis, and facing in the direction you are sliding. Keep centered on the soles of your feet, and equal pressure from your boot cuffs on your shins and calves. Drag both pole tips to help you balance. For added difficulty, use a Javelin stance, with the inside ski lifted and your raised leg and ski pointing in the same direction as the belly button. Develops balancing in a stance that has an oblique angle between the pelvis and legs and skis.

5) Garlands, two or three shallow turns one way, then a full turn the opposite way, and repeat. CAUTION: watch uphill so you don't interfere with other sliders and riders. From an angled traverse as described in drill #4, let your skis turn a little uphill, then briefly slip sideways to point downhill before the next little turn up hill. Minimize turning the pelvis; concentrate on turning the upper legs relative to the pelvis to perform the drill. After two or three turns in one direction, do a full turn and repeat in the opposite direction. Develops turning the legs without turning the pelvis and upper body, and maintaining a steady center of pressure while the legs turn.

6) Falling leaf. Sliding forwards and backwards while slipping sideways to mimic a leaf drifting downwards to the ground, while keeping your center of pressure as steady as possible. Stand with knees as apart as the skis, with most weigh on the downhill ski, and belly button aimed across the toe-piece of the downhill ski. Use the sides of runs that slope

up from the regular run, or the fall line on a gentle groomed run. For more difficulty, raise the uphill ski, which forces you to balance fully on the downhill ski. Develops balancing with precision, keeping the center of pressure steady and within a small target area.

7) Braquage. Straight line of travel down the hill with upper body and pelvis turning as little as possible while skis and feet alternate left and right, slipping sideways most of the time. Hold your poles near vertical and both pole tips scuffing lightly along the snow. Use a groomed blue slope; the exercise is more difficult on flatter terrain. Develops turning the legs without turning the pelvis, while maintaining a steady center of pressure.

8) Smooth skidded turn to stop, punctuated by a pole plant (note: plant the pole after you've stopped, otherwise you can trip yourself up!). Start as in drill #3. Be sure your belly button aims across toe-piece of outside ski during and after stopping; preserve your coiling. While stopping, gaze at least ten feet ahead in the direction of travel, looking across your outside toe-piece. Do not look down. Plant the outside pole just after the skis stop sliding. Use this every time you come to a stop. Excellent blending drill that patterns turning while maintaining a steady center of pressure, and coiling.

9) Javelin stops. Same as drill #8 but with the inside ski raised off the snow, the inside knee and ski both pointing parallel to the belly button laser beam. Maintain obliqueness of pelvis and downhill ski during the stop, which will be easier with a conscious effort to pull the sternum over the downhill toe-piece. Plant the downhill pole just after the stop occurs. Develops balancing over a steady center of pressure while evolving geometry to adjust ski grip, and coiling.

10) Bend and stretch. Flex shorter while releasing from each turn, then extend while the skis pick up the new turn, in order that your viewpoint (eyes) flies at a constant height above the snow. Use on roads. Develops the ability to flex and extend while maintaining a steady center of pressure.

11) Sliding 360's. On a smooth gentle slope, travel straight downhill while spinning around in consecutive 360's. Choose flat, gentle slopes with lots of room. Hold your feet side by side on the magic carpet, and be sure to keep them there; don't let them wander. Turn your head to look straight downhill for a visual reference, except briefly while your skis are facing

uphill. Do not look down. Develops managing the location of the feet, and using the powerhouse to help balance.

12) Straight line of travel while skis link arc to arc. Drag both poles to leave two straight lines in the snow, and turn the upper legs in order to have the skis leave clean, linked arcs. While turning the legs, concentrate on steady equal pressure on shins and calves, trying to have the outside ski travel close to where the corresponding pole tip is scratching along the snow. Use on roads or wide open gentle groomed runs. Develops turning of the upper legs without turning the pelvis, while maintaining a steady center of pressure.

13) Clean edge to edge arcs on one foot, the other leg holding its ski about a boot height above the snow. Extend the arms to help balance and keep a forward bend in hip joints. Use plantar tension to engage the whole sole of the foot you are standing on to ensure that you are centered on the corresponding ski. Tilt the ski by turning the upper leg and standing on the side of the foot that the ski is tilted towards. Turning the upper leg adjusts the edge angle, and balancing on the corresponding side of the foot completes the movement. Keep the raised leg relaxed to make it easier to turn the leg you are standing on. Use on roads or wide open gentle slopes. Drag both pole tips to increase stability and success while learning. Develops agility, balance, and awareness of the turning action of the ski due to turning of the upper leg.

A final comment on practicing and working particular objectives is to mix it up: vary speeds and turn sizes within the same run. Do a few carves, a few skids, a few slipped out turns, and repeat. Often, alternating between easy/slow and challenging/fast allows accelerated practice with a given focus, seeking to feel when it is 'right' versus 'wrong'. To improve, we want to work with a given focus in situations that offer enough challenge that 'wrong' occurs sometimes, yet not so often that realizing 'wrong' and correcting to 'right' is out of the question. Once we succeed with a given focus at a given level of difficulty, we can further develop it by pursuing it in more demanding circumstances; on steeper or rougher terrain, at higher speeds, or at a higher cadence, i.e., more quickly from turn to turn. With experience, repetition develops neural pathways that make trained movement patterns automatic. Automatic allows us to focus on what we want to achieve and less on how to achieve it, so our skiing advances from difficult work to unfettered play.

INSIGHTS

This section delves into topics introduced earlier to provide deeper understanding of how they relate to skiing well simply. They are consolidated here to serve as a handy reference, as well as a means to avoid the key messages in previous sections getting buried in an avalanche of words.

Tactics for Balancing

One characteristic of skiing is the prevalence of underfoot 'turbulence' that acts to shift our feet around under us. Such turbulence doesn't occur when standing still on solid ground, earthquakes excepted, but is prevalent when skiing. Consider what standing in a canoe on a wavy lake would be like. Your feet would get jostled up and down and side to side, not unlike what happens when you ski over uneven terrain. In the canoe, you would need to accommodate this jostling and at the same time keep balancing and rebalancing, or get wet.

You would likely employ several tactics to avoid making a splash, and that serve equally well to balancing while skiing. Standing with feet at a comfortable width, neither too close together nor too wide apart, would give you a platform to balance on, like the magic carpet. Extending your arms out to the sides and front would be likely; picture where a circus performer holds their arms, or consider where you would instinctively hold your arms when walking along a log. Looking ahead, rather than down at your feet, would give you a sense of where horizontal is, and augment other balancing inputs, such as the inner ears, and proprioception, particularly from the feet and ankles. Allowing mobility in the hip joints would help you keep your upper body, the bulk of your body mass, steady. A steady upper body provides an inertial base for movements, and a steady vantage point for viewing and assessing what lays ahead, both positive contributors to balancing successfully.

There are differences between standing in a rolling canoe and skiing during a turn. One is that the mid turn geometry for skiing well simply has our legs and feet pointed obliquely to where our pelvis faces, to the right during a turn to the right, and to the left during a turn to the left. Another is that, unlike bobbing around on one spot, we are in motion, so have momentum. Momentum makes balancing easier, since we can make movements that result in our feet moving side to side under us, an option that is absent when standing in one spot. Consider how much easier it is to balance on a bicycle that is rolling forward compared to when it is stationary. Whenever we sense we are toppling, we steer into the direction in which we are toppling in order to correct our balance. When skiing, the equivalent is a subtle pointing of the knees by turning the upper legs relative to the pelvis. A fractional turn of the upper legs in the direction of the upcoming turn causes our skis to grip and turn, as long as we are standing centered and balanced. Another major difference is that when skiing, having momentum leads to big swings in how much we weigh; heavier during turns and when impacting bumps, lighter between turns and when hopping dips. My instantaneous weight can easily exceed double my static weight at mid turn and drop to zero when airborne. Such significant changes in weight encourage me to adjust my stance within a range of alignment and geometry in which I can resist heavy induced weight yet be relaxed enough to move quickly. Our alignment and geometry is largely dictated by the angles in our hip joints, which are set and managed by the strength and mobility in our primary engine, the powerhouse.

The Powerhouse and Skiing

How well we employ the powerhouse determines how simple our skiing can be. Why do I say this? The powerhouse contains significant mass that contributes momentum, movement that drives geometry and thus ski grip, and strength that resists the weight increases that result when the skis grip and turn. This tight coupling of movement to geometry to loading, plus the strength and mass embodied in the powerhouse, makes the powerhouse our foundation for skiing. I'm much more concerned about how effectively I engage my powerhouse than what I am doing to my skis, arms or poles. Effective use of the powerhouse is prerequisite to skiing well simply, given its major influences on momentum, posture, ski grip, and mobility. At the center of our body, with its movement and strength controlling whatever grip we accomplish on a slippery footing, it is the foundation of our skiing.

I've often seen students and instructors preoccupied with peripheral concerns, such as where to hold the hands, how to plant the poles, how much to bend the knees, how to 'roll' the ankles in order to edge the skis, etc. These topics are secondary to having our powerhouse in order. If our powerhouse is poorly arranged, engaged, utilized, or oriented, our foundation for skiing is flawed. A flawed starting point can only mean a long road to perfectly flawed skiing, somewhat akin to a golfer developing a swing so ugly that only their mother could love it, persisting with that swing because it has become familiar and 'feels right' through its repetitive use. The same phenomenon applies to skiing. A skier with a poor foundation for skiing, i.e., poor use of their powerhouse, will practice and ingrain suboptimal movements. As a result, their on-snow experience falls short of its potential, and worse, their acquired style (or lack thereof) poses a visual workplace hazard for ski instructors. "Your skiing makes my eyes hurt" comes to mind! How many people do you know who worship powder days, but miss many excellent ski days because they lack the knowhow for safe carefree fun in less than ski-magazine-cover conditions?

The powerhouse is the foundation for skiing well simply, in all conditions, with each turn being the first best turn of the rest of your life. Alignment begins in the powerhouse, and effective alignment during the turn helps us resist loading while relaxing enough to balance through nuances and disturbances. Alignment and balance lead to effective geometry that ensures our skis grip and perform throughout the turn while we balance, and to coiling which enables smooth flow to the next turn. The powerhouse is central and formative in the overall process.

The Powerhouse and Balancing

Our powerhouse plays a key role in our balancing act, especially amid the turbulence that arises through our feet while skiing. Recall the canoe on a wavy lake scenario. Add in the possibility that the inside of the canoe is covered in slippery oil, and you can immediately sense your core and legs working to keep you upright on this rolling slippery platform. Kind of like being on a pair of skis, except when skiing, our skis provide grip in the lateral direction and our ski boots provide emergency support in the fore and aft direction. Even with our skis gripping solidly, our feet often get jostled in the fore and aft direction, such as when our skis punch through deep then shallow pockets of snow. The powerhouse contributes strength and reflexes to balance amid these variations. Its strength sets and maintains the geometry of our stance which contributes ski grip during a turn. Its reflexes help us rebalance on an ongoing basis, more readily when we are aligned and relaxed.

The optimum for reacting and balancing during a turn is standing with no more tension than needed to stabilize, standing mostly on the arch side of the outside foot on a strong outside leg, while otherwise being fully relaxed. Relaxation allows reflexes to work, quite unconsciously, as they would to keep us upright in a slippery canoe, to react automatically to correct minor imbalances. To deal with major balance challenges though, we need to tap the strength that controls the flex in our hip joints.

That strength is primed to act if we remain within good skiing postures. Good skiing postures include a forward bend at the hip joints; during the turn that forward bend plus obliqueness of pelvis to skis encourages grip and turning action of the skis. This same forward bend primes stabilizing muscles in the powerhouse so that they are ready to fire quickly when needed.

Firing quickly is paramount to avoiding crashes, since skiing at even moderate speeds creates fast acting forces. In the fore and aft direction, a sudden slowing of the feet could buckle us forward at the hips, and a sudden jetting of the feet ahead make us straighten at the hips and fall backwards. Either of these challenges can be countered by quickly tensing in the powerhouse to maintain the forward bend in our hip joints. When we maintain our stance as such, any slowing of the feet gets corrected automatically when a braced midsection relays the momentum of our upper body into pressure on our shins, which pushes our boots and skis ahead so that we stay centered. Conversely, any jetting ahead of the feet presses our boot cuffs into the backs of our legs, which gives us something to pull against in order to regain centered balance. Either correction requires quick-acting strength in the powerhouse to hold or adjust the corresponding flex in our hip joints, especially when heavy forces are present.

In the lateral direction, loss of balance starts us toppling to the left or right. This is best dealt with by tilting the skis into the direction we are toppling in order to correct our balance, akin to rebalancing when riding a bicycle. To tilt the skis in given direction, turning the upper legs to point the knees in that direction is very effective since it can be done quickly and is a movement that, by itself, won't upset our balance. The corresponding movement, knees moving horizontally relative to the pelvis, draws on strength and mobility in the powerhouse to turn the femurs in the hip joints. Note: turning the upper legs is very effective for edging, as discussed in detail later in this section. See Edging.

Another balance challenge is sudden changes in the height of the snow that we are sliding over. If we encounter a sharp rise or bump, and want to remain in contact with the snow, we'll need to shorten our stance quickly; of course, taking flight off the same feature is an attractive option when it is safe to do so. Conversely, a dip may call for extending our stance when we wish to stay in contact with the snow. Flexing shorter and extending taller involves bending and straightening in the hip joints as its primary movement, and draws on the powerhouse for related strength and mobility, plus reflexes for ongoing balance.

Alignment and Geometry

Our stance, or how our torso, arms, and legs are arranged relative to each other, relates to alignment and geometry. Effective alignment minimizes the muscular effort needed to maintain our stance amid the loading of a turn, and effective geometry compels our skis to perform the turn while we stand centered and balanced. For me, the perfect turn is when my skis perform the turn as predicted, whether the turn involves carving, skidding, or a combination of both, in return for me standing centered and balanced on my feet. Effective alignment and geometry makes turning a balancing act, rather than a turning act. My movements relate to balancing on a steady center of pressure and accommodating the change in direction that my skis deliver, rather than twisting, turning, rotating, or otherwise making a turning effort in order to force my skis to change direction.

Our skis turn, or, carry us along a curved line of travel, provided they grip the snow in the lateral or sideways direction enough to cause a turn to happen. The main determinant of grip and turning action of our skis is their tilt on the snow relative to the direction that our weight presses down through them, or, their tilt relative to the direction of our weight vector. From earlier in BALANCE, our weight vector is an imaginary line that runs downward through both our center of mass, the equivalent of all of the mass of our body plus clothing plus equipment, and our center of pressure, a single point that represents the center of where our weight presses through our feet. Ski tilt relative to weight vector is set by the geometry of our stance, which is led by the angles in our hip joints.

Ski Tilt and Grip

The amount of tilt on our skis largely determines the type of turn they perform, or, how much they slip sideways while they execute a turn. Very little tilt encourages a lot of sideways slip and typically leaves wide shallow smears in the snow, or wide blown-out swathes in deep powder. More tilt encourages more grip, less slip, and more speed, as the ski pursues a carved turn, leaving clean grooves in firm snow or a trough in deep powder.

Grip affects how readily a ski slides lengthwise rather than slipping sideways to the direction it is pointed in. In general, the grip of a ski dictates how effectively it deflects our line of travel into a curve. With grip, we can choose to travel a curve we intend at a speed we intend. Without grip, we are strictly at the mercy of momentum, and ultimately gravity. At times you may have witnessed the 'phantom luge', a skier sliding straight down a steep slope on their back, feet first, devoid of poles and skis. The head-first on-back version, 'inverted skeleton', is also a popular variation on this theme!

Grip is a function of the tilt of the ski relative to our weight vector and the softness of the snow. Usually the ski needs to be tilted a little more than perpendicular to the direction of our weight vector in order to curve our line of travel reliably and predictably. Grip plus pressure from our weight bends the ski lengthwise which causes it to carry us along a curved line of travel; that curved line of travel is a turn. Note that forcing the skis to swivel into a new direction is turning the skis, but doesn't necessary constitute a turn. A turn only occurs while our line of travel is curving to the left or to the right, which is the result of grip.

<u>Geometry of Stance and Ski Grip</u>

The geometry of our stance sets the tilt of our skis relative to our weight vector, and can markedly affect the grip and turning action exhibited by our skis. If we stand ramrod straight with feet straight ahead and level on the snow, our skis sit flat on the snow and our weight presses perpendicularly to their bases and to the snow. With the skis thus, they offer no grip on the snow, and readily slip sideways, exhibiting no turning action. If we adjust the geometry of our stance to tilt the ski without changing our center of pressure, the ski will become more reluctant to slip sideways. Its reluctance to slip sideways reflects the ski's grip. Figures 27(a) and 27(b) help explain these concepts.

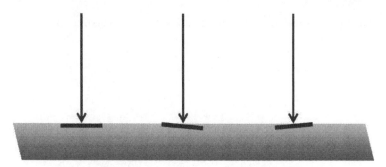

Figure 27(a). Three examples of a ski on a level area of snow, viewed as a cross section looking along the length of the ski. The vertical arrows indicate the weight vector, the horizontal lines the cross section of the ski underfoot, viewed from the tip or tail of the ski.

In Figure 27(a), the leftmost image represents a flat ski and a neutral, relaxed stance. This is the desired tilt of the skis for properly fitted ski boots when standing neutral; attention boot fitters! The middle and rightmost images represent the result of changing geometry of stance while balancing on the same center of pressure. When the ski is tilted relative to the weight vector, it will tend to slip towards the side of the ski that is tilted into the snow. In the middle image, it would slip to the right and in the rightmost image, to the left. Note for later reference that these two images show tilts of five degrees to the right and left relative to the weight vector, respectively.

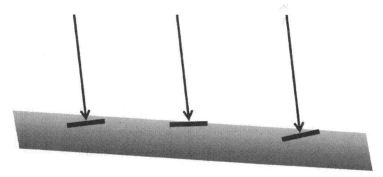

Figure 27(b). End views of a ski during a turn, with the weight vector inclined in accordance with balance.

During a turn, our weight feels like it is acting downward, even though a photograph of us skiing will show us inclined, or tipped, towards the inside of the turn. Our inclination is a result of us standing balanced, rather than due to us tipping our bodies towards the inside of the turn. Figure 27(b) shows our weight vector tilted accordingly as it might be during a gentle turn. Whatever the inclination, the grip of a ski is primarily due to its tilt relative to the direction that our weight acts down through it, and secondarily by the snow conditions. In the leftmost image, the stance is neutral, with the skis perpendicular to the weight vector. Here, the skis usually grip a little, more so when the snow is soft enough for the waist of the ski to sink deeper into the snow than the tip does. The waist penetrating more deeply than the tip adds lengthwise bend to the ski, which, when inclination is factored in, results in a curve in our line of travel. In deep powder, inclination-driven tilt is usually enough to produce a turn. In the middle image, the ski is likely to slip sideways towards the outside of the turn, 'surfing' across the snow rather than cutting into it. In the rightmost image, the tilt of the ski relative to the weight vector makes the ski press deeply into the snow on one side, and provides a very positive grip. Here the ski will tend to bend lengthwise readily and perform a turn with more carving than skidding or slipping. Note that the firmer the snow, the more precisely we must judge how much grip is needed, and how much effort or movement is needed so our geometry drives sufficient tilt to compel our skis to turn as we expect and intend. Finally, the harder the snow, the more it matters that our skis have sharp edges in order to ensure positive grip and turning action.

With all grip and no slip, a ski will carve a turn, leaving a narrow groove as its tail tracks exactly the line traveled by its tip. When a ski carves, it slides purely along its length so that friction is close to zero; hence, carving is conducive to higher speeds. When a ski skids, it still travels mostly lengthwise, but also a little sideways. Its sideways travel plows some snow and dissipates some energy, so skidding allows us to control and reduce speed. When ski slips, it tends to slide about as much sideways as forwards. Its tilt on the snow is minimal so it surfs across the snow, rather than plowing and pushing snow, so it offers minimal grip and braking effect, and, very little control over our line of travel: very disconcerting! If you've skied a hard snow day on a wide pair of skis with dull edges, you know the feeling. Allowing our skis to slip is useful in varied terrain, and the ability to mix carving, skidding and slipping gives us the versatility to ski many types of slope and snow condition.

Whatever grip, skid or slip we intend, our skiing will be its simplest when we stand with a geometry that we can maintain while our skis react to how they are tilted by that geometry.

In summary, effective alignment and geometry leads to our skis performing a turn as we intended they would, in return for us balancing over a steady center of pressure while they do.

Effective Mid Turn Geometry

I seek a stance geometry at mid turn that holds my skis tilted to grip and turn, yet is sufficiently aligned to help resist the loading of the turn. At mid turn, the pelvis facing across the outside ski is a consequence of turning the legs to match the change in direction made by the skis. Such turning of the legs develops an angle between the direction of the skis and the direction of the pelvis. Why this is an effective and desirable mid turn arrangement becomes apparent when we understand how forward flex at the hip joints relates to ski tilt and grip.

Figure 28 depicts the basic effect on ski tilt from bending at the hip joints while staying balanced. Any bend at the hip joints, assuming an in-balance condition, will cause a corresponding tilt on the lower legs that the ski boots then lever to the skis. The diagram characterizes the effects when the skis are turned a full 90 degrees to the direction of the pelvis. Geometrically, the tilt to the skis will be according to the cosine of the angle between the directions of the skis and pelvis. At an angle of 30 degrees (5 minutes on a clock face) the tilt calculates as half of what it would be at 90 degrees. Given the parameters in the diagram, a tilt of 7 degrees relative to the weight vector is possible within readily achievable stance geometries. Such stance-geometry-driven tilt produces a marked effect on the grip of the skis.

A benefit of this pelvis-feet obliqueness and forward bend in the hip joints (while centered and balanced) is a reliable grip on my skis. Keeping my center of pressure steady requires my feet to move ahead throughout the turn, involves flexing forward at my hip joints which tilts my skis relative to my weight vector and thus enhances their grip. This boosts confidence since the odds of an edge slipping out or my skis otherwise ceasing to grip late in the turn is much reduced; all I need to do is balance while the turn progresses, and let my stance develop obliqueness while the skis perform the turn. In essence, I get some edging for 'free', or at least 'included' for the price of balancing with obliqueness between skis and pelvis throughout the turn. In this life, few things are free, but many things are included. This is one of those things.

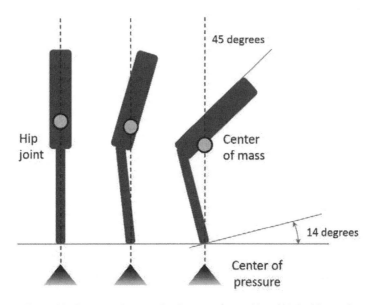

Figure 28. Conceptual connection between forward bend at the hips and tilting of the skis. This diagram shows an example where a 45 degree forward lean of the upper body forward at the hip joints causes a 14 degree tilt on the skis, provided the feet are turned sideways 90 degrees to the direction of the pelvis. The tilt to the skis is according to the cosine of the angle between the skis and pelvis, so at a more likely angle of 30 degrees, the tilt to the skis would be 7 degrees. Notably, the pelvis being square to the skis reduces the amount of tilt from bending forward at the hips joints to zero; hence, the value of preserving obliqueness late in the turn.

Edging

Setting the geometry-driven tilt on our skis so they produce a turn as intended is our basic target for every turn. When we predict the grip we need, and arrange the geometry of our stance to achieve it, the skis turn while we do little more than balance on our feet. Of course, we may not judge or execute perfectly every turn. Besides, the snow condition can noticeably affect the amount of tilt required to achieve a turn of a given sharpness, all other factors being equal. On hard icy snow, the tilt usually must be greater to achieve a given lengthwise bend and sharpness of turn. In soft deep powder, the tilt can be less than on hard snow, since the pressure of our weight causes the middle of the ski to penetrate more deeply than the tip. This underfoot penetration amplifies the lengthwise bend and reaction of the ski. If you have ever gotten going too fast in deep powder you may have discovered that it is quite tricky to slow down without linking several somersaults together! In sticky or uneven snow, the ski's tip may tend to grab and change the direction of the ski more quickly than normal. A required skill for skiing well in varied conditions is edging.

Edging means controlling the amount of tilt on our skis readily and quickly while staying centered and balanced. Skilled edging rolls the skis side to side, adjusting their edge angle relative to our weight vector, without shifting our center of pressure. Notably, I want to edge my skis without interfering with balancing or coiling, so I need to move in a manner that adds or reduces tilt on my skis without me shifting my upper body around or turning my pelvis as part of the move. If I cause either of these to happen while moving in order to change the tilt on my skis, it would make both balancing and coiling more difficult.

My preferred edging move is turning the upper legs, without turning the pelvis, in order to point my knees in the direction that I want to tilt my skis towards. Turning my legs to point my knees to the inside of the turn adds tilt and grip, and turning my legs to point my knees towards the outside of the turn reduces tilt and grip. Turning the upper legs moves the knees side to side, which rocks the lower legs side to side, which, by virtue of our ski boots, rolls our skis side to side. For me, the knees moving sideways about one inch changes the tilt of my skis by three degrees, which noticeably affects their turning action. From earlier, geometry of stance provided about double this amount, which validates using geometry-driven tilt to set baseline grip, and fine-tuning the tilt and grip by turning the legs relative to the pelvis to further drive ski tilt and grip, and especially when the snow surface is hard, tensing the outside foot so as to pronate it to the extent the ski boot permits.

Turning the upper legs to affect ski tilt is fast, strong and minimally disruptive to balance, geometry and coiling. Turning the legs is familiar; it happens with every turn. During alignment, turning the legs slightly in the direction of the upcoming turn tilts the skis so they grip and begin the turn. That slight turn of the legs is a continuation of uncoiling between turns so happens readily. A little extra leg turn increases tilt and grip, and a little less leaves the skis flatter on the snow. The same move can be done at any point during the turn to increase grip or increase slip, and provide versatility to deal with uneven and variable terrain. Notably, turning the upper legs happens with every turn, and using a little more or less of a familiar movement keeps learning as simple as possible.

There are other possible movements for edging the skis, but I find that turning the upper legs provides excellent versatility, dexterity, and holding power. I've seen two other methods for edging taught on many occasions, each with its weak points, as follows.

One is 'roll your ankles'. Trying to corkscrew the feet inside stiff ski boots in search of a big increase in ski tilt is difficult and ineffective. This move at best augments the tilt that is driven by the bigger muscles higher in the body, rather than causing those body parts to adjust because of the effort in the ankles and feet. At worst, implementing this suggestion tenses the ankles, feet and lower leg muscles, wasting effort and interfering with proprioception and balancing. This method uses parts of the body that are better utilized for finesse and fine-tuning; an analogy would be using only the hand and wrist to swing a tennis racket.

The other is 'bend at the waist', or, bend somewhere in the midsection of the body; there's usually a big lack of specificity with this guidance. Bending in the midsection involves the powerhouse, which is better at providing structure than moving quickly. Manipulating the powerhouse shifts significant body mass around, which moves our center of pressure and complicates our balancing act. It also takes a lot of effort to perform quickly and is hard to gauge how much movement to use and do. It is a big body movement to achieve what a lesser body movement can achieve more quickly and precisely, and has the added disadvantage of disturbing our balance.

Thankfully, turning the upper legs taps strength in the powerhouse to adjust the tilt of our skis effectively, quickly, and precisely, with minimal challenge and complication to balancing and coiling.

Boot Alignment

Geometry-driven ski grip works best when our boots are properly aligned. Boot alignment is strictly an equipment issue, and belongs at the top of our equipment checklist. Properly aligned, our boots should hold both skis flat on the snow when we adopt a neutral stance with knees aimed straight ahead. In addition, we should be able to flex and extend our overall stance over a significant range without feeling our center of pressure move in the fore aft direction.

Flat skis when we stand neutral relates to lateral alignment of the boots. Refer to Figure 29. If the bottoms of the boots are not level when standing on the magic carpet with feet straight ahead, the skier will need to compensate in some manner. Knees pinched together or feet wider apart than the hips suggest that the boot soles and thus skis are tipped outwards when the skier stands neutral. Bow-legged stances, with the knees wider apart than the skis, indicate the opposite. Here the boots are holding the skis tilted inwards, already a little 'edged', when the skier stands neutral. This causes the ski to want to grip too much in a turn, which prompts the skier to reduce the grip and reaction of the ski by standing a little bow-legged. In either case, the skier is poorly aligned, standing awkwardly and working harder than necessary. Over time, bad alignment can lead to muscle strains and imbalances. Provisional adjustments can be made on-hill to neutralize the tilt of the boots. One approach is inserting something such as trail maps between the sides of the boot cuffs and inner liners of the boots in order to level the bottoms of the boots. Another approach is under-boot shims, as long as they are thin enough not to interfere with safe operation of the binding. The real solution is to have an astute boot fitter align the boots properly, which should be done at first opportunity.

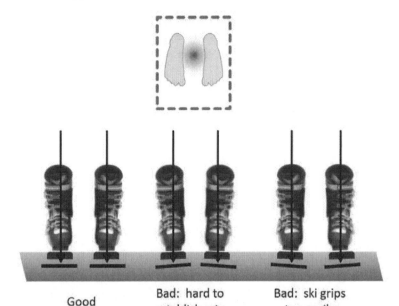

| Good | Bad: hard to establish grip | Bad: ski grips too easily |

Figure 29. Face on views of skier's boots and ski bases, when standing on skis on snow that is soft enough for the skis to tilt according to the alignment of the boots. The ski bases being anything but equally level signals that a boot cuff adjustment or some other alignment fix should be carried out at first opportunity. Inserting plastic wedges under the heel of each boot in order to flatten the base of the ski can sometimes be an on-hill adjustment.

Flexing vertically over a steady center of pressure relates to fore-aft alignment. When skiing, we should be free to flex and extend our stance over a significant range without having our center of pressure shift ahead or back, or, without relying on our boot cuffs to hold us up. The greater the range, the more readily we will be able ski on 'the foot the whole foot and nothing but the foot'.

The main determining factor is the forward lean that our boots and ski bindings hold our lower legs in when we stand centered in our boots with our skis on a flat surface, feeling equal pressure on our shins and calves from the cuffs of our boots. The right amount of forward lean should place the kneecap vertically above where the toes adjoin the foot, which represents that the knee joint is properly positioned over the ball of the foot. If the knees are too far back, with the lower legs quite upright, flexing to a shorter stance will require deeper bending at the hip joints and likely a sore lower back. Conversely, if the knees are too far forward, with kneecaps perhaps ahead of the toes, the legs will be too bent to withstand a lot of weight, putting a lot of strain on our quadriceps. Figure 30 shows the factors that contribute to the forward lean of the lower leg. Figure 31 shows the effects of too much or too little lower leg forward lean on a skier's posture and what they might look like from the side when extended tall or crouched low.

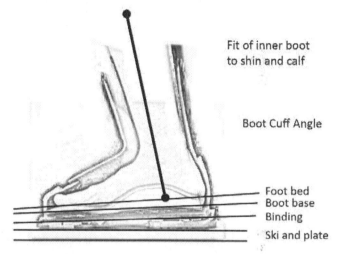

Fit of inner boot
to shin and calf

Boot Cuff Angle

Foot bed
Boot base
Binding
Ski and plate

Figure 30. The factors that dictate the forward lean of the lower leg. The relative height of the ski binding under the ball and heel of the boot, the boot ramp angle as a combination of the boot base and foot bed, the forward cuff angle of the boot, and the stiffness and fit of the padding around the leg all contribute. Notably, raising the heel with internal shims as a tactic to make the boot fit more snuggly, as well as bulging calf muscles, can both contribute to excessive forward lean.

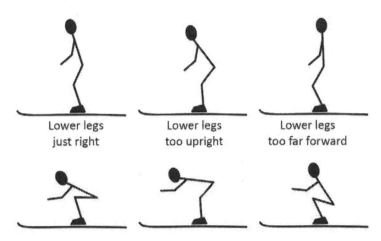

Lower legs
just right

Lower legs
too upright

Lower legs
too far forward

Figure 31. When the knees are near straight above where the toes meet the foot, then the forward lean of the lower leg is likely about right. The test is whether you can extend tall and crouch low while maintaining a steady center of pressure. When testing, be sure to be clipped into your ski bindings and move only as far as possible before significant shin or calf pressure against the boot cuffs.

In terms of snugness of fit, the boots should prevent the feet from sliding forward or backward or side to side, yet hold them securely without any pressure points, numbness or cramping. Importantly, a little ankle flex must be possible; the knee should be able to move fore and aft at least about an inch without an air gap developing between the lower leg and boot cuff, and, the lower foot should be able to roll a tiny amount, just enough to assure proprioception, which is essential to balance reflexes. There should be no noticeable heel lift when pressing gently on the balls of the feet using a little plantar tension. This combination ensures that any shift away from being centered and balanced in the fore and aft direction immediately generates pressure against the cuffs of the boots, which helps shift the skis to where centered balanced is restored. Boot fitters, take note!

Where Not to Stand

Seeking to stand on the 'whole foot', while intuitively obvious, seems less widely adopted than one might think. In discussions with other instructors, and when teaching people who have taken many lessons in the past, using the whole foot and nothing but the foot, and especially, not pressing the shins forward into the boot cuffs, seems new to many. The high rate of success of the 'whole foot and nothing but the foot' in my own skiing and with students satisfies me that it is very effective at all speeds and in all situations, so I wholeheartedly embrace it in order to ski well simply.

Other alternatives that I have encountered as being the 'right thing' to do or what I 'should do' or 'should teach', but that I consciously choose not to, include the following:

"Stand on your heels and press your shins into your boot cuffs. Pretend you are squeezing an orange between the top of each foot and shin, so you feel pressure on the top of your foot and your shin, and weight on your heel." My thoughts: having trialed this for a period of time, I see unnecessary effort with no advantage over simply standing and balancing on the soles of the feet, using the sensations of the boots against the lower legs and feet as confirmation of centered balance. I question the logic of doing otherwise in light of how the human body is designed to balance.

"Press your shins into your boot cuffs to pressure the tips of your skis early in the turn, and then feel your weight shift to your heels by the end of the turn." My thoughts: pressing on the shins invokes a rebound of the boots at some point in the turn, which pushes the feet ahead and risks getting thrown into the 'back seat' late in the turn; on your heels with the back of the boots rammed into your calves, or worse, lying prone in a heap. Seeking a shift in where weight is centered fore and aft seems unnecessary. It also adds risk with no reward, especially when the loading of the turn is significant.

"As the turn progresses, seek to feel the center of your weight move from just behind the ball of the foot to just ahead of the heel." My thoughts: while purposely moving your center of pressure around may help develop balancing and re-balancing skills, it is optional in the context of simple effective skiing. Weight acting downward through the middles of the feet ensures that it also acts down through the middles of the skis. A steady center of pressure simplifies the reactions of the skis, which makes it easier to maintain balance.

"Good skiers can ski with their weight moving around on their feet, and do whatever is necessary to stay balanced. Hence, there's no need to be concerned with where the weight is on the soles of the feet." My thoughts: athletic ability can compensate for a lack of a steady center of pressure, but I believe that athletic ability and a steady center of pressure contributes to the ultimate simplicity in skiing.

I've worked with each of these alternate approaches enough to be able to perform them, yet remain convinced that the 'steady whole foot' approach is more robust and easier to perform, and leads to simpler skiing. I use plantar tension to keep the ball through the heel of the outside foot engaged throughout each turn. Plantar tension is a bit of a mouthful, and you may have heard 'step on the gas pedal', a near equivalent that usually means press down on the big toe or somewhere on the front of the foot early in the turn. How hard to press, and whether to press down with the toes, is quite unclear. Here's the missing clarity: press on the ball of the outside foot just enough to ensure both ball and heel are carrying weight, and work to avoid a buildup of pressure on either the shin or calf of the outside leg, throughout the whole turn.

Grip and Obliqueness of Pelvis to Skis

Recently I realized that my tendency when approaching a challenging situation, such as an upcoming compression on a big mogul, was to turn my pelvis in the direction that I expected my skis would turn, just before the compression arrived. Doing so might have been protective instinct to avoid plowing head on into trouble. Unfortunately, turning my pelvis reduced the tilt and grip of my skis, resulting in a rhythm-killing skid rather than a turn-finishing grip. This led to needing to inject special effort to get the next turn to start, either more leg turn or some upper body rotation to help force my skis into the next turn.

I see this flaw often in other skiers, turning the pelvis into the direction of the turn before the skis grip and begin to perform the turn. Even a slight turning of the pelvis in advance of when pressure builds in the turn reduces the grip and turning action of the skis.

Why does turning the pelvis into the turn reduce grip on the skis? Because doing so reduces or eliminates the geometry-driven ski tilt that is achieved through obliqueness between the pelvis and skis. The better approach is to keep the upper body facing the challenge, or facing the action, and to move the feet ahead to deal with the impact of an upcoming mogul. That will keep your geometry encouraging the skis to grip and turn, thus preserving your flow.

Coiled Torsion: Where in the Body?

Coiled torsion gets distributed to some extent throughout the whole body. However, some parts of the body are better suited than others for building and releasing torsion and thus should be our focal point for coiling. The parts we enlist should be able to absorb and rebound a twisting force without pain or injury, while providing sufficient torque to contribute effectively. Candidate focal points for coiling are: the spine, the hip joints, the knees, ankles and feet. Let's consider each one at a time.

The spine? No. Twisting in the spine while subjected to the loading and extra weight that accompanies turns invites discomfort and injury. Think of bending to pick up a heavy object that rests just a little to the right of your right foot. If you twist your shoulders towards the object without turning your pelvis, lifting it means lifting with a twisted spine. Worker safety guidance says a definite no to simultaneous twisting and lifting, so why would we deliberately ignore that while skiing? When skiing, our spine may need to carry double or triple the weight of our upper body, especially when skiing at speed. Consider piggybacking someone who is your weight. Would you want to carry them while your spine was twisted, with shoulders turned relative to the pelvis? Ouch.

The knees? No. The knees flex mainly in one plane only, although they do accommodate the lower legs rotating a little when the knees are bent; consider how easily you can rotate your lower legs left and right when sitting on a chair with skis hanging freely. The knee joints may accommodate some twist, at least when bent to a deep angle, but the knee has little strength when bent as such. For that reason, and since any thought of a twisting knee joint triggers a corresponding queasiness, knees aren't the place to target for building and releasing torsion.

The ankles and feet? No. These extremities contribute a little torsion, but are not strong enough to serve as a center for storage and release of torque. Besides, we need the ankles and feet for finesse movements with which to fine-tune our balance, especially between turns.

The hip joints? Yes. As the hub of the powerhouse, the hip joints are surrounded by strength and mobility that allow safe strong storage and release of torque. The hip joints also lead geometry of the stance and grip of the skis, which affects turn shape and loading, both which factor into coiling. The loading of the turn works to flex the body more deeply towards the end of turn which allows more lateral and rotational flex in the hip joints and facilitates deeper coiling. Conclusion: the powerhouse, centered in the hip joints, is the best part of the body suited to storage and release of torsion.

Coiling and Flexibility in the Powerhouse

How flexible do we need to be at the hip joints in order to coil effectively? I've seen people who are very flexible in the hips and core from practicing yoga. Watching them contort into different poses is inspirational to watch, though, for me at least, painful to contemplate. Interestingly, these same yogis can have a hard time allowing the necessary freedom of movement in the powerhouse to use coiling effectively in their skiing. Flexibility is an enabler rather than an assurance of skiing-effective geometries.

Equally relieving is to know that the range of flex for good coiling need not be painful. Yes, it helps to be able to achieve about a forty-five degree angle between the pelvis and upper legs, or, in clock-speak, both knees pointing anywhere between ten thirty and one thirty considering the belly button as twelve o'clock. Whatever angles we can achieve, more important is being able to turn our upper legs with equal freedom to the right or left without triggering any turning of the pelvis. Symmetry contributes to better skiing.

Coiling is 'Pre-Rotation'

With the right amount of coiled torsion at the end of a turn, the next turn seems to start automatically. Consider that with no uncoiling assisting the start of the turn, a typical bad move is to rotate the shoulders into the direction of the turn in order to torque the legs and swivel the skis accordingly. Coiling develops the same kind of torsion that results from rotation, but builds that torsion in the previous turn rather than in the current turn. Thus, coiling is 'pre-rotation', with torsion already present when releasing out of the previous turn. Interestingly, coiling takes less effort than rotation, since it exploits the turning action of the skis and the loading of the turn to build torsion in the powerhouse. All that's needed is to preserve that torsion through the release from the turn to enjoy its help in aligning for the next turn.

Moves that Signal Poor Coiling

Effective coiling in one turn means helpful uncoiling torque to help start the next turn. When a skier doesn't have the assistance of uncoiling torsion, they must work harder to have the skis grip and turn as desired. Typical moves that emerge with poor coiling include:

1) Rotating the upper body into the new turn. When a skier turns their upper body into the direction of the turn, it usually signals they want more direction change than they anticipate or than they are getting from their skis. Upper body rotation often follows when obliqueness between pelvis and skis, key for good coiling, is absent during release from the turn. Enough obliqueness through release will encourage the skis to carry the feet across under the upper body to where the skis readily begin the new turn due to the skier's weight and balance alone; here, turning of the upper body to help the skis change direction should be unnecessary.

2) Twisting and bending the spine. Bending sideways at the waist to increase ski tilt is often coached as 'feel the pinch', that is, try to bend so the abdomen gets pinched between the downhill side of the rib cage and the corresponding corner of the pelvic bone. Besides being awkward to do, bending in this manner, which involves twisting and bending in spine, is risky given the presence of turn-driven loading. I've experienced very little change in the grip of my skis, but a lot of back pain from following this misguided advice.

3) Pushing the downhill foot out to the side. I've often seen less skilled skiers push their downhill leg out to the side as a way to get a grip; possibly for the sake of feeling safer, seeing their foot and leg braced between them and the valley below. And, so they can get a good strong push with their foot, they often rotate their upper body into the direction of the turn before thrusting downwards to achieve a safe-feeling braking action. Unfortunately, they are left with the upper body square to their skis, which works against achieving grip. Little or no grip means that their skis don't carry their feet across and under the upper body during the transition, so the skier must again rotate their upper body into the next turn. The result: a self-perpetuated struggle.

4) Actively pressuring the skis. With poor edge angle and grip, another common reaction is to pulse downwards with the legs and feet, by extending and then landing hard on the skis, hoping that a brief

increase in pressure will coax the skis to grip and turn. When the snow is soft enough that the middle of the ski sinks deeper than its tip, a pulse in pressure adds bend and turning action to the ski, albeit briefly, and somewhat precariously with regards to balance. While an option, this movement requires extra effort, disturbs flow, and complicates balancing. A better practice is to develop geometry that drives ski tilt and turning action through effective alignment and steady balance.

Releasing From the Turn

Releasing from the turn triggers our transition to the next turn. What is the simplest way to release and take advantage of coiling to achieve a smooth flow into the next turn? From before, obliqueness between pelvis and skis assures that momentum of the upper body and momentum of the feet and skis drive the switch, leading to a balanced stance going into the new turn for very little effort. The aim is to preserve the obliqueness between pelvis and skis while releasing from the turn so there will be helpful torsion available to assist with alignment and preparation for the next turn during the latter part of the transition. Generally, the shorter the turn in terms of elapsed time, the greater the angle of obliqueness, as shown in Figure 32.

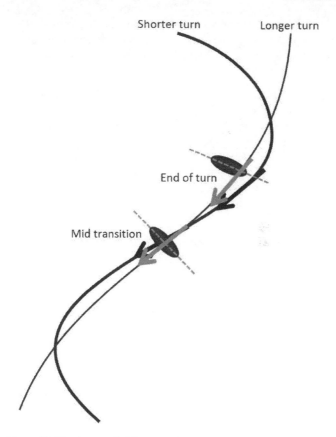

Figure 32. The degree of obliqueness between pelvis and skis varies with the size and openness of the turn. Tighter or shorter turns require more obliqueness since there is less time for the skis to carry the feet across and under the upper body to where simply balancing on the new outside foot produces grip and the start of the next turn.

Release involves letting momentum take the upper body towards where it will be when the next turn begins, while briefly maintaining tilt on the skis so they carry the feet across and under the upper body during the transition. The skis carrying the feet from out to the side to directly under the upper body produces an upward acting boost on the skier. The goal is to leverage this upward boost to achieve a period of light weight in the latter part of the transition; that light weight interval will allow uncoiling torque in the body to contribute freely while preparing for the next turn. Some management of pressure underfoot to achieve what is needed from the upwards boost usually benefits from shortening the stance while releasing from the turn.

Shortening the stance involves flexing at the hip joints and knees. Flexing at the hip joints during release means also brings a visual cue into play: my viewpoint travels straight towards the start of the next turn, which I experience as flying straight towards where I want to be viewing from when the next turn begins. I often picture pulling my sternum forward and along the direction of my belly button laser beam during release. This combination of visual path and pulling forward assures continued ski grip to drive the switch, and coiled torsion to help me align going into the next turn.

Alternate Method to Switch from One Turn to the Next

A commonly prescribed method for transitioning from one turn to the next is to reduce pressure on the outside foot and increase it on the inside foot. The analogous movement and feeling is akin to working a stair climbing machine at the gym. The effect is to switch the orientation of the body from where it is balanced in one turn to where it is balanced in the next turn.

This approach causes the body to topple sideways between turns, the feet being the fulcrum point of that toppling. With the body toppling sideways, a subsequent action is then required to halt the toppling and reestablish balance by early in the new turn. Rebalancing involves pressure on the new outside foot by early in the turn to slow and halt the sideways toppling of the body.

Contrast this approach with a momentum-driven switch in which there is no real loss of balance. In the momentum-driven approach, the fulcrum point, or the point around which the body reorients, is essentially the center of mass. The center of mass is near the middle of the body, rather than under the body, so the body flow is akin to rolling like an airplane, rather than toppling like a tree. While the switch progresses, the goal is to establish balance on a center of pressure that suits the new turn, rather than doing that plus halting the toppling of the body.

One advantage commonly espoused for the stair climber approach is a better alignment for stronger weight-bearing, since it doesn't rely on an oblique angle between the direction of the pelvis and feet. After all, weight lifters don't lift weights when standing with both feet turned to one side or the other. The claim is that square to the skis is required to stand strong.

The ability to withstand loading of the turn is certainly necessary in skiing. However, strong stances are not limited to those in which the legs are straight ahead in the direction of the pelvis. An equally strong stance can be achieved with the legs turned a little to the pelvis, as long as both feet are where they can readily resist weight. Try doing a squat with your legs and knees facing straight ahead, the pelvis square to the legs and feet. Then repeat with both legs (and knees and feet) turned so the feet and knees point five minutes either side of twelve o'clock, where the belly button points. Still strong?

Another espoused advantage is that the switch can be achieved without needing the legs to turn relative to the pelvis. After all, some people have a real challenge flexing rotationally in the hip joints. If their goal is to ski well, however, they simply have to learn the movement. I've seen very few cases of a physical impediment preventing the movement; it is more than likely something the person has simply never tried or done before. Fortunately, the movement is quite learnable.

An obvious disadvantage of the weight shifting approach is its lack of versatility. Shifting pressure on the feet may work on harder snow, but is problematic in powder snow, where pressuring one ski versus the other encourages the newly weighted ski to dive into the snow and induce a tumble. On-piste aficionados seeking to master powder take note! Contrast this scenario with using obliqueness and momentum to drive the switch. A momentum-driven switch works equally well on hard snow and in deep powder. Using a single movement pattern for all situations and conditions means simpler all situation skiing. It is quite satisfying to ski through alternating stretches of soft powder and firmer snow using the same movement patterns.

The Pole Plant: When, Where, Why

A frequent topic when teaching is the pole plant. People want to improve their pole plant, believing a good pole plant will improve their skiing. I agree that a good pole plant is helpful, but only within the context of good alignment, geometry and balance. A good pole plant follows from, rather than leads to, good solid skiing.

When in balance, the need for a pole plant is quite minimal. Holding the outside pole within easy reach of the snow and poised to be planted is highly recommended. This ensures the upper body is oriented quite vertically in the side to side sense, which contributes to effective geometry. I use a rule of thumb to hover the tip of the outside pole close to the snow early in the turn, within a boot height off the surface of the snow. This helps keep my upper body aligned and symmetrical to my pelvis, as in, arms extended forward and out to the sides, and shoulders parallel to my pelvis, with no twist in my torso and spine.

Just after release from the turn, a simple downward jab with the outside forearm touches the pole to the snow. Thereafter, letting the pole swing back as I pass where it touched, without dropping my hand, completes the movement. I seek to move as little as possible and thus minimize any disturbance to my posture and balance. Large arm movements move more body mass around and can affect balance, evidenced by arm swinging that occurs occasionally in order to help recover balance. Quiet arm movements both signal and encourage better balance.

<u>Face the Action</u>

When skiing, as in many other sports, the body is led by where we look. To achieve an intended line of travel, whether skiing or performing a drill, good advice is to look along the line that we intend to travel in order to influence our actions accordingly. Consider skiing through a glade, where trees are interspersed with open snow. Which do you think would be better, looking at what you want to avoid, in this case the trees, or looking at where you want to travel, that is, at the spaces between the trees? Maybe it's just me, but I prefer the latter.

Predicting what we expect to encounter and feel in the next couple of seconds helps us to prepare for whatever awaits. When I am skiing, whether fast or slow, I find it best to scout ahead several seconds for a general plan, then study closely the snow that my feet will slide over about one to two seconds from now, or the time interval within which I can affect where my feet will actually travel. I call this focusing one 'action interval' ahead. By continually watching for and predicting the upcoming 'action', I am better prepared for a positive encounter.

In moguls, the action is where my feet will engage the next bump. On a groomed run, the action is where I'll encounter the next terrain change or where in the next turn my weight will increase noticeably. My approach is to have my pelvis aimed squarely towards the action at all times. That puts me in a good postural relationship to the forces that will soon be acting on me.

<u>Momentum, Speed and Effort</u>

Momentum is tightly linked to speed; physics states that momentum is mass times speed in the current direction of travel. Our mass changes over a period of weeks or months so can be ignored; our speed is really what we are talking about when considering momentum. We can gauge momentum by judging our speed, through vision or by feeling apparent wind on our face and hearing it in our ears, but we can only feel its effects when we oppose it.

Left to its preferences, momentum will carry us in a straight line. As speed increases, it requires greater effort to change our direction of travel or slow down. Deflection, a result of balancing on a gripping ski, pushes our mass sideways to the direction of our momentum, and friction, the result of balancing on a skidding ski, reduces our speed while energy is dissipated in the form of a rooster tail of flying snow, a cloud of chiseled ice crystals, and in ground breaking conditions, a hail of sparks.

That it takes effort to change momentum explains why you see skiers (or snowboarders) traveling straight and fast with seemingly no effort. That is precisely the case. Going straight and fast takes no effort; it is the easiest thing to do, especially on wide equipment that provides a lot of surface area to stand on. Turning and slowing down is what takes effort, more effort the faster the speed, and, the wider the equipment. When you see someone flash by making no turns or making very long open turns, don't erroneously conclude that they are skilled or strong. Conclude that only when they turn or slow down with good control and in balance. If otherwise, call the speed police. Fast does not confirm skilled.

<u>Summary Advice on Skiing Improvement</u>

Other than finding a competent instructor or coach to guide you, and keeping your body fit at least to a moderate level, here are several recommendations to help you improve your skiing.

Start with a good boot fit and alignment. Check lateral alignment; the soles of your boots should be level when you stand neutral, so that simple standing neutral on the magic carpet holds your skis equally level on the snow. Also, check fore-aft alignment; confirming that, when your boots are clamped into your ski bindings, you can bend and extend your overall stance over a wide range without pressing your shins or calves hard into your boot cuffs.

When skiing, balance on the foot the whole foot and nothing but the foot, being ever conscious of exactly where you feel weight on your outside foot and on your shins and calves. Seek to balance and ride on a steady center of pressure, standing appropriately so your skis create turns, rather than working to force your skis to change direction. Think 'balance and ride' rather than think 'turn'. Look ahead and keep your thoughts simple; go with the flow and seek steady and relaxed throughout.

Internalize the principles of alignment, balancing, and coiling, visualizing the pursuit of these guiding focuses while skiing. Perform drills and exercises suited to your skill level, on whatever terrain you feel comfortable. Focus on no more than one specific element of technique at a time, working with it in different steepnesses and snow conditions.

Visualize when away from the ski hill, recalling the positive sensations and results that you have achieved on the hill. This is a proven method of training and improvement for many sports, including skiing.

Persist in your efforts. Learning requires familiarity with how something feels. New movements, even when they contribute to great skiing, may initially feel unfamiliar and foreign. Persistence will get you to where you can perform such movements reliably enough to realize their usefulness, and enjoy their effectiveness. Mastering what works well for you becomes your skiing.

Finally, enjoy your time skiing, learn from your challenges, and relish your improvements.

Disclaimer and Context

There is no single obvious or 'correct' way to ski, evidenced by the many ways that ski technique is described, taught, and performed. Notably though, approaches can vary widely in their efficacy. Some approaches are effective, others less so. Some pose very awkward use of the body, some very efficient use of the body. Some are simple, others complex. Yet all, usually in some way, contribute to moving the art forward.

Skiing can be complex, especially when approached in a piecemeal skills-based manner or with a poor grasp of the biomechanics that contribute to good simple skiing. We've all heard mention of skills such as balancing, edging, pivoting, pressuring, flexing, steering, turning, sliding, slipping, tipping, timing, counter-rotating, etc. We may also have seen techniques espoused for one situation that proved ineffective in another. A movement pattern honed on hard snow conditions can lack aspects for playful skiing in soft powder and broken up terrain. Likewise, a single-minded focus on the carved turn, often posed as the holy grail of ski turns, leaves a lot out in terms of all mountain versatility. In my view, much of the complexity in skiing stems from naming skills or movements but leaving the student to work out the biomechanics that work best in the context of skiing. My preference is to pursue precise target objectives using safe and effective biomechanics in order to produce the sought-after whole: playful flowing fun skiing.

The model in Ski Well Simply is yet another kick at the can of 'how to'. It is one person's take on skiing, with specific biomechanics to suit the physics invoked by a human in motion while standing on pair of slippery skis, complete with the rationale and logic behind why it works, and vetted through high success rates with students at every skill level. As a summary statement, I am much more concerned about what I do with my body than what I do to my skis.

I have no delusions about Ski Well Simply saying a whole spate of new things about skiing, or that Align-Balance-Coil is the 'right' way to ski. The volume of literature that has been produced over the last century by countless pioneers, experts and career ski professionals assures that avid students of the sport will have seen many of the same topics addressed. Quite likely, some aspects will be familiar, while others will seem at odds with how they are performed or utilized in the skiing process. I am hopeful that the particular focuses and how they fit into a model for effective skiing represents some form of originality, and that paring things down to a small subset of topics offers value to learners and experts alike. I also hope that you enjoy mulling over the insights in this book as much as I enjoyed writing them down.

CLOSING REMARKS

Skiing is all about how, when, and where you stand, and who you're with. Who you're with can easily trump ski technique when it comes to memories and having fun on any given day, but how, when, and where you stand determines where on the mountain you can live those memories and have that fun. And, skiing better with less effort allows you to enjoy skiing more, for more hours, and more days, with countless more opportunities for extraordinary on-hill moments.

The Align-Balance-Coil framework distills skiing to its essence, keeping things simple yet compromising nothing in effectiveness. It is led by three guiding focuses, with timing of movements guided by seeking a smooth increase in underfoot pressure to a maximum at the apex of each turn, then a smooth decrease to a light weight sensation from mid transition to the start of each turn. Whether standing aligned and centered on the arch side of the outside foot patiently waiting for the turn to begin, or balancing on a steady center of pressure while the turn progresses and ensuring that the legs and skis turn sooner than and more than the pelvis does, or preserving coiled torsion through release from the turn, the premise is that there is always a specific target objective that will help trigger the appropriate movements and efforts to achieve it. The trick is choosing targets that match good biomechanics with the physics at play, and that produce the desired outcome from our skis.

The part of the body that is central to all these objectives, the powerhouse, sets the foundation for movements and efforts that underpin our success. As our center of ski-affecting geometry, momentum-defining mass and balance-enabling strength, the powerhouse is our foundation for movement while we ride the slippery platform of our skis. When properly engaged and managed, the powerhouse enables our skiing to become as simple and effective as possible. It drives the structure and geometry of our stance, and thus is central to how, when, and where we stand amid the dynamics of skiing.

How we stand relates to alignment and geometry. Where we stand relates to where we feel our center of pressure to be, as well as the line of travel we choose, predict, and then get carried along by our skis. When we stand reflects the timing of pressure changes we seek turn to turn; the smooth increase in pressure as our skis progress through a turn, and the lightness we experience between turns. The kernel is balance. The sensations we feel on the soles of our feet and our shins and calves provides biofeedback that helps us pursue a steady center of pressure throughout each turn, and feel precisely our quality of balance.

Align-Balance-Coil is the model for simple and effective skiing that I use and teach. At least for the time being. My ongoing quest for the purest simplest maximally effective skiing continues...

CREDITS AND ACKNOWLEDGMENTS

My journey to better skiing is inspired by many trainers and colleagues, most of whom are long time locals in the Whistler Blackcomb ski school and ski racing circles. My appreciation for their honest and open dialog and genuine heartfelt guidance is timeless and ongoing.

I'm thankful to Maureen, my better half, for enduring my distractions of the creative process and the time absorbed by writing. You are a tireless proofreader and willing guinea pig for testing the understandability of what I've crafted.

To my students who listen carefully and then try whatever I recommend, persist with enthusiasm in their learning, laugh understandingly (sympathetically?) at my bad puns, and flash a rewarding smile when smitten by success, I'm forever grateful.

And for the photography in this book: jasonchowphotography.com. Besides having a flair for photography, Jason has a flair for skiing.

Made in the USA
San Bernardino, CA
20 August 2019